Anne,

God's Blessings

any joy on your

way Home!

Fr. Joy Sandahaa

My Greatest Joys on my Way Home

BOOKS BY THE SAME AUTHOR:

ON MY WAY HOME

REFLECTIONS ON MY WAY HOME

MY GREATEST JOYS ON MY WAY HOME

Rev. Jay Samonie

Library of Congress Control Number: 2004092069

ISBN: 0-9752636-0-9

Printed in the United States by
Morris Publishing
3212 East Highway 30
Kearney, NE 68847
1-800-650-7888

6

AUTHOR'S NOTE

My first book *On My Way Home* was written by surprise. I did not intend to write a book; I merely wanted to jot down a few events of my life for my nieces and nephews to read. I saw them relatively often but we rarely discussed anything personal at one of our family gatherings for a baptism, a wedding or a holiday. I thought they would find it interesting to know a little more about their uncle. My books may surprise them as well, reading about my mystical and spiritual experiences, many of them being strange and often odd experiences...compared to an average uncle. I figured that less than thirty pages should be enough to convey my purpose. Yet when I began writing, I did not realize that it takes a certain number of pages to talk about one's life. A lot more than I anticipated!

Very unexpectedly, those supposedly few pages I was going to write turned into an entire book. I was no longer just writing for my nieces and nephews, but for their parents and my other relatives and cousins. Soon I found writing a pleasant experience, even therapeutic, and I began addressing anyone who would like to read my story. It got bigger and bigger. The first book was well received and is now in its sixth printing.

I received an abundance of letters concerning my first book. They were positive and encouraging. I continued writing almost in response to the many letters and their questions about God, life, death, destiny and many other topics. After about a year, my second book was published: *Reflections On My Way Home.*

Again, I received a lot of positive responses in the mail to keep writing. The result? This third book, *My Greatest Joys On My Way Home,* was born...forming a trilogy of books. Was this planned? Hardly! The theme of this third book was being developed as I began to write. As you turn the pages you will see that my greatest joys happened on certain occasions. Not everything we do brings joy to one's heart, but I discovered that reaching out to another in need with a truly selfless and unconditional expression of love does fill the heart with joys that can best be described as heavenly in origin. These, then, are among the greatest joys of my life. I believe that you, as a servant of God, will find it to be true for you as well.

Rev. Jay Samonie

February 27, 2004

ACKNOWLEDGMENTS

My sincere gratitude to Msgr. Clement Kern, who was a mentor and inspiration to me while I was a Seminarian and as the priest following him at Holy Trinity Church in Detroit.

I am also grateful to Reverends Dennis Dillon, S.J., Ezequiel Mondragón, Randall Joyce, CPPS and Sisters Ann Currier, I.H.M., Mary Ellen Howard, R.S.M., Annette Zipple, R.S.C.J. and Margaret Hughes, I.H.M.; Jerez Jackson, Sally Owen, Richard and Kathy Rice, Paul Manion, Shirley Beaupre, Noreen Keating, Jack and Ronnie Morgan, Kathleen Carolin, and Mary Turner.

THIS BOOK IS

DEDICATED TO:

The Staff members of Most Holy Trinity with whom I worked for eleven years and those who came for help and were our teachers as well.

The seventeen members of the original team of Priests, Mexican Sisters, and lay folks that began the organization *Latin Americans for Social Economic Development (LA SED)*. I am also grateful to the first Officers who initially operated LA SED, their present Staff and all the clients and donors that have contributed to making LA SED faithful to its commitment of service to the Hispanic Community for so many years.

The Lighthouse Staff and its volunteers are very much included in my gratitude and

11

dedication for the countless hours of service given to all who called for help.

My uncle, Archbishop Joseph Simon Assemani, and several other uncles/Bishops who served the Church with a life-long commitment since the early 1600s and who have laid the foundation for an important portion of this book being written. I shall continue to hold them in my heart with a deep appreciation.

CONTENTS

13

14

15

PART ONE

HOLY TRINITY CHURCH, A HAVEN FOR OUR HOMELESS AND VOICELESS BROTHERS AND SISTERS.

1. IN SERVICE IS FOUND HAPPINESS!

"I have come to serve

not to be served"

-Jesus

When I consider the many adventures and unexpected situations I experienced throughout my life, I often wondered what brought me my greatest happiness and joy. It was easy to review the important events in my life, such as being ordained a priest, receiving certain awards, completing my Degrees in Education, being excited over my best golf game, finishing a painting, feeling good about a talk I gave publicly or achieving a host of other accomplishments. These were very satisfying moments...and unforgettable. But they were mere *moments* and not a continuous joy to my whole being. Was there something in my way of life that made *Life* worth living and filled my heart with purpose and meaning? Something that would constitute my greatest joys as I continued, day by day, on my path Home.

To my surprise, the answer was staring at me on the door to my bedroom. It was the poster in Spanish, a translation of a verse, authored by the famous Hindu poet R. Tagore. It read:

Dormí y soñé

que la vida era alegría;

desperté y ví

que la vida era servicio

serví y descubrí

que en el servicio

se encuentra la alegría.

To me, it was the key and the secret to true, life-long happiness in this life. Translated, it says:

I went to sleep and I dreamed

that life was happiness;

I woke up and I saw

that life was service;

I served and I discovered

that in service

is found happiness.

Rabindranath Tagore's experiences were far more reaching than mine. His accomplishments were truly phenomenal! Unlimited! He lived from 1861 to 1941. In those 80 years he was knighted in England, awarded the Nobel Prize for Literature, established schools in India, had Art Exhibits of his paintings in Europe and the United States, set 3,000 songs to music, authored about 60 poetical works and volumes of stories, some of which are very famous to this day.

His discovery of finding happiness really got me excited about writing another book. Seen from the viewpoint of actually experiencing happiness, I could not agree with him more. As I reflected and mused over the most fulfilling moments in my life, I came to the same conclusion. Never did I experience more fulfillment and accomplishment than in serving others in my priestly Ministry.

It is a true statement: my greatest joys or moments of happiness came in helping others to cope with life, counseling others, leading others, serving others, initiating programs to improve the living conditions of others or just being there for others. Did I forget about number one on these occasions? Is that what life is all about...just giving and giving till you burn out? Not at all! Life is giving and receiving, giving and receiving. It is a fact that the giver receives more than the recipient. That is why the saying "It is better to give than to receive" is so true.

In my discussions with families, I believe they are saying the same thing. Their whole life is caring for their children and later their grandchildren. Giving complete and unconditional love for an infant is very fulfilling. The infant is totally helpless; the parents feeding, washing, clothing, and the many other things they do for their child results in an extraordinary sense of fulfillment and happiness. As a child grows up, the care is more intense, calling for more sacrifice of time and effort. Yet the *service* parents provide for their children, regardless of the age of the children, carries the same result: a sense of accomplishment, peace and joy.

Who is the head of the household? The one who *serves*! And who are the *servers* in the family? The parents. It seems to be Nature's way of telling us all: "in service is found happiness."

What I have included in this book are my efforts to live by Tagore's suggestion: "I served and I discovered that in service is found happiness," although I did not reflect on what he said until a week ago. At the same time, I cannot refrain from hearing the Lord Jesus affirm: "I have come to serve, not to be served." His words now have a special meaning for me.

2. THE POOR ARE GOD'S TEACHERS.

"The poor you will always

have with you."

-Mt. 26:11

"What do you mean by beating my peo-
ple to pieces and grinding the faces of
the poor?" Says the Lord God.

-Isaiah 3:15

My ultimate years of service took place
in the inner city. Seen from the aspect of
service, this is a story that had to be written.
It was only a matter of time when and how
it would appear in print. There are some things
in life that will never go away. Quite often
the good that is being done in the world is
overshadowed by the negative and the sensational.
And so heinous crimes, monumental accidents
and unprecedented disasters make the front
page headlines in newspapers, while the events
that demonstrate loving service and the thousands

of stories of generous, common folks may never be told. Occasionally, stories of a spiritually enriching nature do find a place in the news, but that is not a daily occurrence.

The focus of this portion of my book is my eleven years of service to the poor and homeless in Detroit, Michigan. Those eleven years, from 1977 to 1988 represent the period of time in which I was the Pastor of Most Holy Trinity Church situated in the heart of Detroit. Actually, I was assigned to several parishes in the general inner city of Detroit for a total of twenty-five years...with no regrets! But at Holy Trinity, I experienced my greatest spiritual enlightenment. Those were difficult, but soul-stirring years and it was a privilege to be there. I use the word *privilege* because I was living among the homeless, who came to our door by the hundreds every week of the year for financial help, assistance, direction and guidance and sometimes, just for a word of comfort or a listening ear.

Though it may sound strange, they were my teachers! In a very true sense, their attitude towards life itself and living the difference between *what we want and what we need* turned my life around. I was being introduced to a world whose existence I knew nothing about. I was prepared to teach the Gospel...I thought. I was not prepared to hunt for a cigarette for someone down to their last dime...or stumble over bodies huddled in front of the rectory door each night. I have always thought and still do that my role is one of *preaching* the Gospels, but this church was already *living* the Gospel at a much deeper level of consciousness. I learned that death and resurrection were a daily occurrence here. Yes, they came to our door and received help, but we all benefitted, both giver and receiver.

Most Holy Trinity Church is situated on the corner of Porter and Sixth Street in the core inner city of Detroit, Michigan. It was the first day of my pastoral assignment, July 1, 1977. I had no idea what to expect. Good thing! If I had known in advance the number of people who would be waiting at the door at 9 a.m. in the morning, I would have changed my mind, turned around, and headed straight out of town. *And miss the lesson of a lifetime!!!*

I believe I am a reasonable person, but there is limit to what an average person can endure. My eyes popped open and my feet tensed up and wanted to run in the opposite direction. There were over fifty faces staring at the front door. I just stood in amazement as about half of them managed to edge their way in and quietly found a spot on the old church pews that lined the hallway of the rectory. As I watched them file past me, I saw *suffering,* but more than that, *I saw myself!*

Not long after that first encounter, I was able to look each one in the eye... and nearly in the state of shock, *I saw the face of Christ walking by me, one by one.*

Most Holy Trinity Church was not just another church where people came to worship. We considered it a beautiful Temple of the Lord and so did everyone who entered her hallowed walls. But it was more than that! Holy Trinity was an *experience* that had become the heart of a city, a beacon of light for the lost, and a comfort to the homeless. There are many ways to describe the life of a Parish Family; it can be seen from a strictly historical viewpoint and well documented with all the facts and data that occur within its lifetime. Or it is possible to view a church such as Holy Trinity through the eyes of real people, who experienced a personal role in its history. This latter approach is the one I wish to pursue and share with you. As the Pastor of Holy Trinity, I lived a full eleven years in the Parish House on Porter Street and Sixth, which is known publicly as *Corktown*. Yes, it was rewarding spiritually but I needed all the creative skills I was capable of, with a firm commitment and a gift of patience that never quit.

Eleven years encompasses much more information and experience than can be put in a single book. Together, with some staff members' input, I hope to offer to the reader some first-hand stories of real people, including those who owned nothing but what they were wearing. These latter ones helped weave the remarkable history of Holy Trinity Parish.

It is rather peculiar that some of life's greatest lessons are learned from those who have very little. Their days are filled with a continual struggle to survive in a troubled world with no hope for a better future. The homeless appreciate the smallest things in life, have very few needs and almost no comfort. These are some of the lessons staring at those who have just about everything they want, but are still not fulfilled. Often *those-who-have* live with the same fears in life, concerns about health and a general feeling of failure as *those-who-have-not*.

Added to the wonderful work that was being done in this little inner city church, *miracles* happened often at Holy Trinity. This is not an exaggeration. There was a documentary on Channel 2 (a major channel in Detroit) by Joe Weaver back in the seventies. It was called, "*The Miracle of Porter Street*," and described the Ministry of the beloved Fr. Kern who was Pastor at Holy Trinity for thirty-four years prior to my Pastorate. A few years later, another documentary by Joe Weaver was aired on the same channel. It was called *"The Angels' Song,"* and focused on the work with the homeless that was being done by myself and my Associate, Fr. Sam Campbell, of happy memory. During my Pastorate, miracles at Holy Trinity continued to occur, surprising us all! And miracles certainly encourage a total giving of self to the spiritual work before you.

Working in the inner city is both challenging and demanding. It is definitely not easy and calls for some kind of philosophy as a foundation for one's convictions. Certain questions have to be answered if one wishes to continue having successful and productive results. Otherwise, it is quite easy to fall into a narrow mind-set of being depressed because of the lack of accomplishment. Perpetual lines of the poor calling out for help with their hands out and insisting on personal and immediate attention can totally drain one's energies.

Having served my first week at this busy hub of activity, already meeting on a one-to-one basis, and trying to bring a glimpse of hope to all who came through our doors, I was actually beginning to enjoy my work. It felt good to serve! It was fulfilling to see the same joy on the face of a man who walked the streets all day and found a helping hand, a willing listener, a friendly smile. This was made easier by the fact that I had spent over two hours talking with my mentor, Fr. Kern, a few days before my assignment there. But having knowledge of what to do and actually confronted with real life problems is quite a different thing. I was ready and willing to do my best regardless of what happened. I discovered that working with large numbers of homeless and powerless members of society is a work of art indeed.

Is it any wonder that Jesus spent time each night alone with His own thoughts and taking time to converse with His Heavenly

Father for encouragement and strength? He spent His days mingling with hundreds and, at times, thousands of poor souls spiritually starved. They were grasping for a blessing, a healing, more of His new Teachings or a positive suggestion to get them through another day. It is not surprising that He too needed spiritual refreshment...but He kept giving and giving!

Jesus did not come to end all poverty in the world nor did He attempt, even remotely, to solve all problems. He left that up to us. "The poor you will always have with you." (Matthew 26:11) Never in the history of the human race has there been a time when poverty was obsolete. And no such period of time appears to be looming in the future. Also, Christ emphasized what was proclaimed in the Scriptures: "To love your neighbor as yourself."

Because the Lord Jesus Christ has endeared Himself to every human being, we, at Holy Trinity, took this mandate literally and welcomed everyone who was in need. Each, without exception, was our neighbor! We put out the word that we wanted to care for those whom no one else wanted! We welcomed, without a previous appointment, anyone who was in need. Such a program was called *The Open Door Policy*. There were many, in particular, who were no longer eligible to be assisted by Social Service Programs. Their only recourse was to fall through the proverbial *cracks in the Social System*. Without pointing fingers, let me just say that the above situation exists in every society. Shangri-la, a paradise on earth, exists at the present time, only in one's imagination or in books such as *The Lost Horizon*, by James Hilton.

Was our role simply to help others without learning anything from that experience? I think not! There were an abundance of lessons to learn from the poor.

It took me a long time to accept the fact that there were so many people living in the United States — a super-power and the wealthiest country in the world — who daily walked the streets and had no place in this world they could call their own. It was difficult to imagine a person being happy without a home, a family, and at least, a minimal income with which to survive. Yet, there are literally many thousands of human beings in America without a roof over their heads, whose lives and whereabouts are unknown by Society.

I am not speaking from imagination about what could possibly happen. I am talking about stark reality! We were confronted each day with the homeless! Each week with hundreds of them! They are people like any other people...except that they *own* only what they are wearing or carrying with them.

It is thought-provoking to think that when they stepped through our doors they were probably experiencing the only precious moment of the day. They were happy to be there. After being warmly greeted by myself or one of the staff, they were assisted to the extent we were able.

Where do the homeless go? What do they do? Where do they rest their heads at night? After all these years, I continue to pause in amazement at their ability to survive. It was not unusual to return to the Parish house after dark and practically trip over a few bodies comfortably resting for the night on our doorsteps or small porch. The first evening I came back from my day-off I did trip and nearly fell. Immediately, a hand moved quickly in my direction! It meant no harm; rather, I would hear that frequently

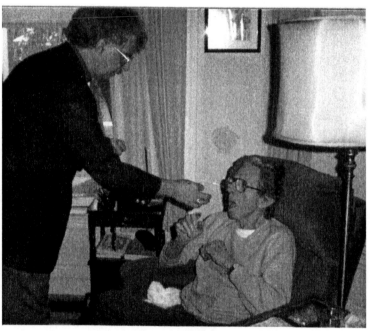

Fr. Jay offering communion to shut-in

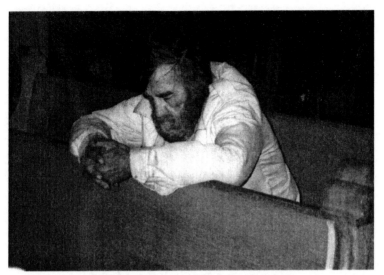

Knight of the Road in prayer

repeated refrain: "Hi, Father, can you spare a buck?"

I learned very soon in my Ministry among the homeless that, for some of them, lying all night next to the door of the Rectory was the closest thing to home and the safest place to sleep for the night. With that in mind, I made no effort to stop them; *the welcome mat* was pleased to witness a few *Knights of the Road* taking advantage of this strange arrangement.

In the winter, however, circumstances changed radically. With unbearably freezing temperatures, it was no longer a haven of security. The men quickly made they way over to Kelly's Mission on Michigan and 18th street or to Salvation Army's Harbor Lights on Cass Avenue. They were given a warm meal and a place to sleep. Still, some of them chose to stay outside all night. One of our regulars who we called *Cowboy*, made such a choice. He would cuddle under the steps of the side entrance, and actually survive one cold night after another.

For a long time I did not know he was spending his nights that way — even in zero and sub-zero weather. With cardboard under him and newspapers over him, he managed to beat the cold.

This was not true of those who were drinking and fell asleep behind some bushes in the alley or out on a park bench. I learned from a friend working in the Rehabilitation Center in Downtown Detroit, that an alcoholic who drinks himself to sleep out in the cold is very vulnerable to end up freezing to death. The alcohol gives its victim a false sense of warmness for the night. They actually do feel warm temporarily, but as soon as the alcohol is absorbed by the body — while they are sound asleep — their bodies freeze very quickly. They never wake up!

The first year I came to Holy Trinity, it was a fierce winter, much colder than usual. Several men froze to death out in the cold. From that point on, we made every possible effort to get the men to a Rescue Mission for the night. The following year only two experienced death by freezing. Only rarely did that ever happen again.

The funeral of a street person was very sad; not only because one of us left this world but also because no one hardly ever showed up. There were no family or friends usually. Many times, the only ones present were Sr. Ann Currier (the Pastoral Minister), Clayton Brundage (the Funeral Director) and myself. Since that became too much to bear, we celebrated their funerals at the regularly scheduled 12:10 p.m. Mass. The majority of those in attendance came from their offices in the downtown area. It was truly a sacrifice, but somehow they managed to squeeze in a quick lunch before getting back to work.

Whenever we had a funeral of a person without a family, the State Police, stationed across the street from the church, volunteered to be ushers bringing the casket into church. You might say that an instant family was established for the deceased and this spiritual bond was felt by all in attendance. It was their gift to the poor!

Regardless of who died, we did not change a single thing. A homily befitting a creature of God was delivered and there was always something good to say about the fellow who wandered the streets seeking a portion of happiness in this world. They also had something else in common: during our counseling sessions, if the topic of *God* came up, I received a distinct impression that they felt God's love and protection. Also, that Jesus had not abandoned them. Theirs was simply a different

38

way of life. My heart was always moved by their sense of enlightenment. I was filled with joy!

I recall on one occasion, we had two funerals, with one immediately following the other. The first Funeral Service was for a wealthy benefactor, the other for one of the Knights of the Road. After both funerals, a parishioner, somewhat confused, came up to me and said: "You practically gave the same talk for both of them. You just changed some of the names!" I replied: "Since God loves all His children with the same Divine Love, I see each of us, regardless of our background, as siblings belonging to God's Divine Family." My role was to serve my brothers and sisters to the best of my ability. Making such judgements on the life of another human being was not my role nor was I capable of doing so. St. Paul even asked his followers to pray for him *lest he himself* would become a castaway. *The person who has achieved perfection* may, like Christ, be in the position to know all the facts about everybody. I was not there!

Even the toughest among the street people loved the picture of *The Laughing Christ* which hung over the fireplace in my office. Of course, we never spoke of religion unless the client brought it up and encouraged the discussion about God, moral values or any religious topic. They were treated as brothers and sisters of Christ. I do not want to give a false impression that they were living a life with high moral values and were shining examples of holiness, but I am saying we never judged anyone; we left that to God's Divine Wisdom.

Holy Trinity Church was a place that welcomed everyone, not just the poor and the homeless, but also clergy who needed a place to stay. During my eleven years as Pastor, every room was taken. There were three floors and it was always filled. Besides myself, there was an Associate priest, a retired priest and two seminarians on the second floor. On the third floor were some of the workers who took care of the front door and phone. Another helped in counseling and still another handled the fund-raising programs. We all had one thing in common: We were there to help...and, yes, to serve!

An Outreach Program of Christian Service to outsiders does not sit in a vacuum, but rather comes out of an activity approved by its membership. Holy Trinity Church membership consisted of a dedicated Christian Community of about 400 families. Their assistance was absolutely essential in accomplishing our work with the homeless. I will address this issue further in the book, but I would like to compliment them from the very beginning for their zeal and cooperation in making it possible to offer help to our brothers and sisters who walked the streets.

3. MY FIRST THOUGHTS

ABOUT HOLY TRINITY

"Kindness is a language

Which the deaf can hear

and the blind can see."

-Mark Twain

Love bears it out even to the edge of doom.

-William Shakespeare

To love means to love the unlovable. To forgive means pardoning the unpardon-

able. Faith means believing the unbeliev-
able. Hope means hoping when everything
is hopeless.

-G. K. Chesterton

My very first thoughts about Holy Trinity began when I was a college student in the Seminary. Several of us students had done some census work for Fr. Kern. That was my first encounter with this wonderful man. I had hoped that some day I would be his Associate working at Holy Trinity. It would be an honor to work side by side with an ideal, priestly Pastor. I could learn so much from him just watching him doing what he did best. He was considered incomparable in the working ethic of total commitment and total service.

Never did it occur to me that some day I would be following Fr. Kern as Pastor, but that was precisely what happened. Following a legendary, accomplished and very well-liked Pastoral leader, such as Fr. Kern, does not help one to develop a healthy, well-balanced self-image. Quite the opposite is true! Following such a huge personality could be overpowering to one with a weak and fragile self-concept! Taking charge of the work done by Fr. Kern for 34 years called for someone who already had a sound and secure self-image. Fortunately, before I accepted the assignment at Holy Trinity, I felt that I was at the spiritual peak of my priestly Ministry. I was forty-seven years old and I felt that I had done it all! My view of life was built on a solid foundation!

I had lived through a wide variety of experiences that ranged from being an Associate Pastor in several parishes to being a Pastor of four different Parishes for almost thirty years. In the Archdiocesan framework, I also held a few active positions: being a Vicar and a member of the Assignment Board for the Archdiocese. I also was Director of the Hispanic Apostolate, a member of the Senate (a forerunner of the present Presbyteral Council), and a Director for Cursillos (weekend retreats) in Spanish, and also sat on a Team preparing

Spanish-speaking Deacons for the Archdiocese of Detroit.

Before I went to Holy Trinity, I had just completed five years as Pastor of St. Michael Church in Pontiac, Michigan. The Parish Council, Staff and myself had envisioned and had just completed our five-year goals in four years! If I had taken any pride in my accomplishments up to that time, the bubble suddenly burst in my face! I was caught off guard! With almost no preparation, I found myself stepping into another world...the world of the voiceless and homeless. It wasn't easy! I had faced many challenges before, but there was nothing in my personal history that prepared me for the unique experience of following Fr. Kern in the inner city of Detroit. His fame and accomplishments extended far beyond the physical boundaries of Holy Trinity.

Imagine following in the footsteps of such a person: About ten years before Fr. Kern made his transition, there was a state-wide poll taken. People from all walks of life and from every background and religion were asked: "Who, in your opinion, is the mover with the greatest influence toward progress in the State of Michigan?" Asking for the most prominent mover in the State would normally place someone of very high rank in first place. The voting surprised everyone! Before the Governor of Michigan, the Mayor of Detroit, and the Cardinal, being the spiritual leader of well over one million members, was this humble but very powerful Pastor I was to replace. Replace? Hardly! He was a one-of-a-kind dynamic individual who God sends into our midst from time to time! He was operating on a level far above the ordinary.

I do not know a single priest who, in his right mind, desired to follow Fr. Kern as Pastor. As soon as I heard that Fr. Kern was going to retire, my famous quote was, "I pity the poor fool who follows Fr. Kern at Holy Trinity!" Little did I know that *yours truly* was going to be that *poor fool!*

My first shock at Holy Trinity was that I had no name...for about three years! Would they remember the name *Fr. Jay?* Not usually!

My name was "the priest who followed Fr. Kern." Even meeting the same people again and again, evoked the same response: "I remember you very well! You're the priest that followed Fr. Kern!"

I thought to myself: *Must I go through that again?* When I came into this world, I was named *Jacob* after my father. And so early in life, as far back as I can remember, my name at home was *Junior.* When I was ordained a priest, my name was no longer Junior! It became *Father.* I still had no name! After a period of time, I insisted that my siblings call me by a name. My sister Jennie, who has since been called to heaven, gave me the name *Jay.* It was perfect. I liked it and have used it ever since.

At any rate, it took three years and a talk by Fr. Kern himself on St. Patrick's Day at Holy Trinity to finally make the change in leadership. He addressed a church filled with politicians, business men and women, dignitaries from the government, the medical field, the church, and a large percentage

47

of the Irish and would-be-Irish-for-a-day present. His presentation was expected to be about St. Patrick and the Irish and the special collection for Holy Trinity's programs for the parish and for the poor. No one could have guessed what his topic would be! It was not about the Irish, St. Patrick or the famous collection better known as *The Sharin' of the Green*. Rather, he focused his entire homily on Fr. Jay as Pastor of Holy Trinity and how successful and effective was the work I was doing since his retirement. He emphasized that if anyone wanted to have him participate in a program at or connected with Holy Trinity, please get Fr. Jay's permission. He is the Pastor! Fr. Kern was so complimentary all through his talk that I wondered at times who he was talking about. After Mass, however, the official change took place: at this point — after three long years — I was completely accepted as Pastor...and with a name: *Fr. Jay.*

While the crowds were making their way slowly out of church, I happened to see two

Fr. Clement Kern

St. Patrick's Day procession

49

well-known Judges standing in front of the doors of the church. I edged my way towards them just to say hello. One of them said, "Well, here comes the new Pastor of Holy Trinity!"

I blurted out: "Excuse me, but I have been Pastor of Holy Trinity for three years!"

"No! Not really! Now, you are Pastor!" And he was serious! With Fr. Kern's public approval, somehow, and in some strange way, everyone just happened to remember my name! That incident describes the power and influence of Fr. Kern and his humility of graciously bowing out of the spotlight. I then became able to serve others with my own, actual name, *Fr. Jay.*

Interestingly enough, several years before I moved to Holy Trinity, I was teaching a Course in self-improvement which included techniques to improve one's self-image. Teaching the Course many times, and making every effort to practice what I teach, I came to Holy Trinity with a fairly strong self-image, so I must say that I was not defeated by all the well-deserved attention Fr. Kern received. I did begin to wonder briefly, at times, if I was making an impact or not, but I knew who I was and I did not want to be anyone else.

When I accepted the assignment as Pastor of Holy Trinity, I insisted that I would run the parish *my way*. I did not want to be the mold of another person, even one as great as Fr. Kern. I taught, for over fifteen years, in my classes on *Mind Development* and *Stress Control* to be yourself...that we are all unique, that each of us has our own gifts and we all have something to say, to do, and to contribute.

My intent was to learn as much as I could from Fr. Kern, who was my mentor, but apply what I know through my own convictions. I never intended to destroy programs that were successful, nor would I continue others that were obviously doomed. Consequently, I kept up much of what I inherited from Fr. Kern. He was creative, insightful and, at the same time, very sensitive in his efforts to assist those who were in need by improvising new

Fr. Jay teaching The Silva Method of Mind Development and Stress Control

and inventive ways to meet such needs. I was not selected by the Assignment Board of the Archdiocese "to come in and clean house." There was not much to *clean*! I believe my values concerning priestly service were in line with those of my predecessor, having previously spent about fourteen years in the inner city at other parishes.

Somehow, I quickly adapted to helping large numbers of people on a one-to-one basis! It was a shock to be there, but the kind of joy that we brought to others, filled my soul with a sense of gratitude and amazement. In fact, it was indeed a privilege to share more deeply in the Lord's work.

It was also quite necessary to be bilingual, since two-thirds of the parish was of Hispanic origin. I loved my Ministry with the Spanish-speaking; it was not surprising, therefore, that my favorite Mass was the one in Spanish each Sunday. I was grateful that the Archdiocese had sent me to Mexico twice, once before ordination to Mexico City and the other after, to Cuernavaca. Both were summer assignments. A third time, I was sent to Ponce, Puerto Rico, for an intensive study of Spanish...also for the summer. Being Lebanese and Pastor of a Parish Community, largely Mexican, Puerto Rican and Maltese, I never took sides, preferring one culture over another. I enjoyed all three cultures, rich in music, family values and, of course, delicious foods.

From the very beginning of Holy Trinity as a Parish Community in 1834, it was, without question, an Irish Parish. And it is still very Irish on St. Patrick's Day! The church becomes so overcrowded that every pew and even the aisles and vestibule are filled with people — and there are still more folks standing outside listening to loud speakers. Many of the Worshipers of every nationality speak of *being Irish for the day*. In reality, and apart from that one day, the actual residents of Corktown had changed radically. It had become a Maltese and Hispanic Community.

Talking to some of the Seniors, they remember full well what happened when the Maltese families began to move into Corktown. This comes as a surprise! The Maltese immigrants were *warmly welcomed* by the Irish Community. It was the Irish in the area who rented to them, and would later baby-sit for them. These stories were repeated by a number of the Maltese families. Mary Macallef, Tony Porter, the Preca Family, the Mirabitur Family, and Mary Gatt are just some of those who told how they were immediately accepted by the Irish families. Service comes in so many forms: The Irish Community serving the Maltese Community!

The Maltese families adapted well and quickly. They operated the local grocery stores while some of them held jobs in the automobile factories. Local stores were important to the community because many of the residents had no cars. While I was at Holy Trinity, the Maltese made up about a third of the parish and participated in every activity and position in the parish. They came here originally *receiving* and became *givers* of their time and talent.

There were many challenges in every department of parish life. We had a lot of work to do and our work day consisted of long hours. Yet, left on our own and without outside help, we were financially crippled. We were far from being self-supporting. It was either simple coincidence or part of a Divine Plan that I happened to have the largest Mind Development and Stress Control class in my 16 years of teaching the Course. The classes took place at St. Paul's Retreat House in Detroit, Michigan. Over 300 persons attended. That is extremely large for a class! Twenty to fifty was considered an excellent attendance at that time. The big help came from the Michigan Catholic Archdiocesan newspaper. The front page was divided in half: the top half was a picture of Pope John Paul II who was chosen as the Pope and successor of St. Peter. The bottom half of the page was a picture of myself teaching the Mind Development and Stress Control Course.

Hundreds of callers responded to that wonderful article. I figured that it was a gift from above, so I donated the entire profit to the Open Door Policy Program. From that point on, money was always put aside to lend a helping hand to the financially impoverished. Prior to donating a portion of every class I taught, I discovered that my *wallet* was the *parish fund* for doling out money to those in need. Obviously, helping the people who came to our door each day ended when our wallets were empty.

Fund-raising was a necessary part of my assignment. We actually received only enough donations in the Sunday collection to stay open for a little more than a month. The conclusion was obvious: without outside help, the Open Door Policy at Holy Trinity Parish would not exist and the poor would no longer be served.

Fortunately, God smiled on us. I was overwhelmed by the generosity of people everywhere from all levels of Society. There was never a mail-delivery day without one or more donations in the mail waiting to be given away before sundown. I became more and more elated each day as I witnessed the care-giving qualities of the affluent...and the not so affluent. And the *miracles* continued! We thanked God every day for sending us so many volunteers and benefactors! And the response to our fund-raising projects was phenomenal! All our projects continued to expand so that we were able to meet our parish expenses, although we operated on a year-to-year basis. We thanked God for inspiring so many people to serve in so many ways!

4. CHANGES, LARGE AND

SMALL,

DID NOT COME EASILY.

No great person ever complains

about lack of opportunity.

-Ralph Waldo Emerson

As the new Pastor, every change I made caused a stir. Actually, that was not surprising! For nearly three and a half decades, Fr. Kern was the spiritual leader of the *same* Parish Community. He baptized and married most of the faithful and they were pleased with his method of leadership.

"Who is this guy who has no name — *the priest who followed Fr. Kern* — to come in and make changes like that?" Every little thing I did seemed to be monitored. For instance, when I installed a *live person's* voice to answer the phone late at night — this was not a machine, but a real person — I received a flood of calls opposing such a move. I felt that we needed a full twenty-four hour coverage on the phone.

Naturally, complaints were filed against me to Fr. Kern himself. However, Fr. Kern, in his wisdom, knew quite well that full coverage day and night for every day of the year was practically impossible, especially when there was only one priest on hand. Or when Fr. Kern himself went to Mexico for a month every year! At the time I installed the live answering system, I had been alone a lot, especially when my Associate, Fr. Sam, got ill. After he was re-assigned, I was completely alone for more than seven months. One day, when Fr. Kern was having lunch with us on his way to the Attorney Grievance Committee meeting, he gave his expected response to this whole issue. He simply said to me:

"You are the Pastor. Do what you think is right!" Today, twenty-seven years later, there is hardly a rectory, office or home without an answering machine. And with very few of them having a *live* voice! Again, serving others takes on many forms.

Little changes made big waves. Often actions and events of very little importance upset some of the most active parishioners. Almost any new activity would cause some people to become unhinged! The above installing an answering service was only a simple example. I always felt right about the changes I made. Fr. Kern was still my mentor. Only twice in the six years prior to his passing did I go out to St. John's Major Seminary to visit him: once for advice, and the other for a discussion about a very serious situation that developed at Holy Trinity.

In the first instance, I had made a decision and simply wished to include his input. There could be some strong unexpected opposition from people offended by my ethics. The situation was clear, the result unclear! The Young

Communist Party wanted to use our Hall (Cafeteria) for a large gathering of their membership preparing to spread their propaganda. It was not easy for them to find a place for their propaganda, so they appealed to Holy Trinity for permission to use our facility. At that time, anti-communism was very strong. I had no idea what the consequences would be. It was a policy of Holy Trinity to accept people as they are. We tried to serve everyone with an open mind. Was this the same? I wasn't sure. Regardless, I was moving in the direction of allowing the Communist Party the use of our Hall in spite of a few parishioners' verbal opposition.

At the same time, I was well aware that a huge indiscretion could be disastrous. So I called Fr. Kern. I knew he had faced many delicate situations in his long Ministry. When I explained the apparent dilemma to him, he hesitated only for a moment and gave the answer I more or less expected.

I recall him saying in so many words: "Everybody has heard about the American way and the advantages of a democracy. Shouldn't Communists have a chance to offer their views on a way of life, giving people a chance to hear both sides?"

That was enough for me! So I let the Communists with their propaganda have their day! The result? Not much. A few murmurs, but the local Community saw no serious cause for being perturbed.

The second visit with Fr. Kern, sometime in 1980, was a very important one for the spiritual well-being of the Parish Family of Most Holy Trinity. Unfortunately, the nature of our conversation was confidential. I can only say that, once again, Fr. Kern supported my decision. Guidance from the Holy Spirit also helped, I am sure, and all went well! In fact, my fears of what might have happened were dispelled quite rapidly and unexpectedly.

One day during lunch — Fr. Kern often ate with us at least once a month — I asked him, "Clem, why did you stay here at Holy

Trinity for so long? I am sure you could have gotten another assignment very easily."

He surprised me with his answer. "I chose to come here *at first*. The work was very hard and challenging *but I stayed on because nobody else wanted it.*" I laughed.

He assured me it was true! But he added, "You know, after about fifteen years I began to like it. So I stayed as long as I could." He did, until retirement!

I smiled through our whole conversation. I realized the same was true for me. Not the number of years, but after about five years as Pastor in this inner city parish, I actually began to like it. I really wanted to remain at Holy Trinity until retirement, but my health began to fail, which was hard for me to accept.

I thought my health was invincible. I had been an avid skier, having gone to Aspen, Colorado many times and also skiing out East in upstate New York and Stowe, Vermont. I also spent a three-week trip skiing through the Alps in Europe, skiing in Germany, Austria and Switzerland. I played racquetball, a rather strenuous game, most of my life until just a few years ago. I was no longer vulnerable; I would remain in good health for years to come. Well, obviously, I am not a prophet!

In 1986, I had developed some serious heart and blood pressure problems. How could this happen? I was too healthy! I have been called to serve others! Regardless of what I thought about myself, *I passed out a couple of times,* falling flat on my face both times...the same evening! When I appeared at the altar for Mass the next morning, everyone thought I had been in a fight with one of the clients. It was hard to explain in a way they would believe.

I went to the doctor the very next morning after Mass. After having a thorough check-up by my doctor, he concluded that my blood pressure was unusually high, there occurred a weakening of the heart valve, and the adrenal glands were not functioning properly when I tried to get up out of bed. This was the doctor's diagnosis. *The cause, of course, was stress.*

With the doctor's help, my condition improved somewhat. Nevertheless, three years later, my uncertain and struggling health led to my being re-assigned.

5. SUCCESS WAS NOT OUR GOAL.

"We are not called to be successful;

We are called to be faithful."

-Mother Teresa

How swiftly passes the glory of the world.

-Thomas Á Kempis

Mother Teresa was always a great inspiration to me, especially while I was working in the inner city. Some days, life was more difficult than usual and success seemed so very far away. When more than one project failed in the same day, it called for a second look at one's efforts. It strikes the spirit quite heavily. However, there is no such thing as failure if we are faithful to our goals by not allowing the physical to overshadow our spiritual commitment and accomplishments.

There was a copy of Mother Teresa's words on my desk. It was in the right place! I needed to be reminded often that success was not our destiny. Loving God and being faithful to His word was the true mark of spiritual success.

The life of Jesus was also a good demonstration of being true to the Word of God. Jesus met opposition almost everywhere, but He remained faithful even to His death on the cross. Some Bible Scholars now believe that the words of Jesus: "My God, my God, why have you forsaken me?" were the first words of Psalm 21 and it begins with a despairing cry and ends with a joyful victory. Rabbis at that time often quoted just the first line of a Psalm and everyone knew what was to follow. On the cross Jesus may well have referred to His relationship to God the Father with unconditional love and obedience...as His final words.

"Father if it is your will, take this cup from me; yet not my will but yours be done." (Luke 22:42)

"Doing the will of Him who sent me and bringing His work to completion is My food." (John 4:34)

"I seek not my own will but the will of Him who sent me." (John 5:30)

Jesus remained faithful in spite of daily trials and mockery by those in authority. He upset their world by exposing their hypocrisy and performing miraculous works to support His mission. They, in turn, after opposing Him for three years, finally achieved the opportunity in a mock trial to provide false testimony and to have Him put to death. He was crucified...in obedience to God's Will. Was Jesus successful? Yes, and His accomplishments were multiplied many times over because He served *faithfully* to the very end. What followed was the most incredible event that ever took place on this planet: the Resurrection, the Risen Christ, the Cosmic and Universal Christ, the Glorified Christ. He was truly the Son of God, the Lord Jesus Christ!

St. Paul had similar troubles ever since he was knocked off his horse and converted to Christ's Teachings. We know Paul was shipwrecked, beaten, whipped, imprisoned, scorned and rejected many times. He had every reason to give up, throw in the towel and declare: "I've had it! I want no more of this!" But Paul remained loyal to his Master and Lord. In return, God remained faithful to St. Paul's commitment and granted him a persevering faith and the gift of curing illnesses of every kind. Paul was sustained and strengthened in spirit by the Grace of God. He was, like Jesus, a perfect model of loyalty in service.

We all have the same goal; namely, to love and to serve God by serving others. In this world, unfortunately, spiritual and moral values have been pushed aside in favor of material success, and *keeping up with the*

Joneses is the goal for most *normal* families...none of which is true! This is a great deception, and in this country where capitalism reigns, it is easy to abandon our true purpose of living.

I desired from the beginning of my Pastorate at Holy Trinity to be faithful in serving those in need. That was not easy! Imagine the shock of opening the front door my first morning there and seeing about 50 people already lined up for counseling and assistance of every kind. Each came for a different reason. How was I to know what to do or what to say to each one of them? I had counseled before — many times — but rarely with a person who had no home, was an alcoholic, a drug addict or was drifting along, walking the streets. I was not even sure from the outset what was my *raison d'être,* that is, *my object, my reason for being there!* There was no fund set up to assist others financially, there were no rules, no process, no guide to follow. I relied on my instincts and my natural love of others. Greener than a young oak leaf, but with God's assistance, I continued the Open Door Policy of my predecessor and learned through the very process of lending a helping hand. So, the only preparation I had was simply doing it and discovering my role from experience. Did I want to pack up and get out of what seemed an impossible situation? Yes, I did! Many times! But I remembered the consoling words of Mother Teresa and I was sustained in spirit and purpose.

6. FR. KERN'S LAST DAY WITH US

The true saint goes in and out among the people

and sleeps with them...and never

forgets God for a moment.

-Abu Sa'id

I had written very briefly about Fr. Kern's passing in my second book, *Reflections on My Way Home*. Since Fr. Kern was an extremely popular Pastor and truly a legend in the Archdiocese of Detroit, many people asked if I would tell the whole story concerning the transition of this great man, this extraordinary servant of God.

Within the Parish House of Most Holy Trinity Church, there stands a marvelous antique: an old, solid-oak grandfather clock. How long it has been there or where it came from was

The clock that miraculously chimed

lost in antiquity. There was never a time when it actually worked...never counting the minutes or sounding its chimes on the hour. Yet there it stood stately for many years in the dining room as a silent witness. But that was to change!

August 15th, 1983 was an exceptionally beautiful day! It was also the Feast in honor of the Assumption of Jesus' Mother into heaven. After celebrating Mass in church, about seven or eight of us were just beginning our lunch in the Parish House when, all of a sudden, the clock began to chime. I asked if anyone had gotten the clock fixed. The answer was "No!" on the part of everyone present.

We all looked at each other in absolute amazement as we realized it was Fr. Kern saying goodbye to us. We knew he was in the hospital and that his condition was considered critical, but we were not sure of when he would make his departure to the spirit world. I looked at my watch. The time was 12:47 p.m. We felt strongly urged to go immediately to the Ford Hospital: was Father Kern calling us or was he saying farewell to us and to the place where he had spent thirty-four years of his priestly Ministry before retiring?

Sister Ann said, "Let's go to the hospital...now!" We did! Sister Ann, Terry Garrigan, and I left our food on the table and immediately drove to Ford Hospital. We moved quickly to the hallway marked ICU, where we were met by Leo Derderian, a long time friend of Fr. Kern. From the look on his face, we knew that Father Kern's time had run out.

Standing around the bedside were Fr. Kern's family, a few relatives, the Hospital Chaplain, and the Medical Team attending him. The respirator gave the appearance of a person breathing, but in my heart I felt he had already made his transition. We prayed for a while until they disconnected the respirator. The Medical Examiner promptly stated that Fr. Kern had expired. The Good Shepherd had called him Home.

I spoke to the doctor who had come to examine Fr. Kern's body which he had designated for science. The doctor said two things to me: first, after looking at his watch, he agreed with me that Fr. Kern may very well have died around 12:47 p.m...the moment the Rectory clock had chimed. Secondly, he said that there were no parts of his body that science would want.

This was not surprising to me. After all, Fr. Kern was practically *in constant motion* until his accident on the freeway that put him in the Hospital in the first place. This same doctor affirmed that they could not use the corneas of his eyes, his heart, his kidneys, or anything else that could help another human being to survive. Fr. Kern was so busy serving others throughout his life, that he completely wore out his body.

My understanding was that he survived the accident, but lying *totally inactive* in the hospital for so many days, actually caused his death. In that motionless state — as the doctor expressed to me — his entire vascular system had broken down. In a very real sense, his continuous, active Ministry extended his life.

The result was that *we did have the body present* at his funeral instead of a memorial Mass. Without question, it was indeed the largest funeral that ever took place in the history of Most Holy Trinity Church. Besides the great following of lay people Fr. Kern had, there were many others standing outside who could not fit into the church proper.

There were nine Bishops and several hundred priests.

After hearing the story of the clock calling us to Father Kern's bedside, Mr. Archer, then owner of the Excalibar Restaurant, was so deeply impressed that he said he would be willing to pay whatever it cost to fix the clock. James Pickard, a specialist in repairing grandfather clocks, was hired to do the job. He made some very interesting statements to us. He maintained that it was absolutely impossible for the clock to work and still more impossible for the clock to chime off the hour.

He presented us with clear evidence: there were no parts in the clock to make it function! Also, it was built only to chime on the hour; besides, those parts were also broken. After spending a great deal of time putting the clock together with new parts, it now faithfully ticks away and chimes the hours.

The whole incident of being witness to a miraculous farewell by the spirit of Fr.

Kern has still left us all in a state of wonderment. Every person present (and still living) will testify to this surprising, but awe-inspiring experience.

7.SHADES OF DAMON RUNYAN

When man is all wrapped up in him-
self,

he makes a pretty small package.

-John Ruskin

Sometimes Silence is not golden...
just yellow!

-Anonymous

I also learned a lot about fund-raising.
Generosity was often found in the most awkward
places. As I became more familiar with the
kind of people who were instrumental in keeping
Fr. Kern's wallet filled from day to day,
along with the support and fellowship he
needed to meet parish expenses, I kept telling

myself that some of these characters came
right out of a Damon Runyan story. *Guys and
Dolls* by Runyan was one of my favorite stage
plays...and movie; characters played by Frank
Sinatra and Marlon Brando are real city people.
So were Fr. Kern and some of his friends.
Leo Derderian was the owner of the Anchor
Bar where politicians, television, radio and
newspaper celebrities, governors, priests
and the like gathered often. And we cannot
overlook Chickie Sherman, a bookie, or Maxie
Silk, who ran a Deli where the gang, including
myself, were often seen having breakfast.

These personalities could have starred
in any of Runyan's stories. They were a classic!
And there were many more! Out of such a group
originated the famous *Shakedown Society,* in
which undue pressure would be put upon Leo's
clients to donate to Fr. Kern's work with
the poor. They actually passed the basket
in the Bar...just like in church. It worked!
I am sure that some of the men sitting at
the Bar — after a few drinks — did not know
how much they generously donated to the Open

Door Policy of a church down the street which they never attended. Chickie enjoyed shaking down the pockets of his *clients* as well. You might label their work: *serving with force.* I, too, spent many hours at Leo's Anchor Bar, being treated to the best hamburgers in town! I met practically every one of those customers who were *urged strongly* to donate to the work of Holy Trinity. Not one of them regretted for a moment what they donated, sober or otherwise.

After Fr. Kern was called to heaven in 1983, I worked more closely with Max Silk. Max fit well into our kind of thinking...and believing. He was Jewish, but having an open mind, he had many Christian friends. Most of his clients were Gentile Christians, like myself. Did that matter? Not in the least. Max attended our celebrations at Holy Trinity, even our religious ones. He would bring green beer and braided bread on St. Patrick's Day. He even attended the Mass on that day.

An interesting thing happened when Max turned eighty years old. He arranged to receive the bar mitzvah ceremony that I thought was reserved only for a young Jewish lad. In attendance at the Temple was a full congregation, about one third Jewish and about two thirds Gentiles. I enjoyed the whole thing, especially when the Rabbi asked Max why he did not receive the bar mitzvah when he was a young man. Max responded a little red-faced. "Rabbi, when I was a young man I was in jail, a member of the purple gang!" The entire congregation burst out in laughter. We had another big laugh when Max sang certain scriptures in Hebrew. His pronunciation we were not sure of, but there was no mistake that he did not carry a tune very well. It didn't matter. We loved him and nothing could change that!

In the process of keeping such company and being strongly influenced by them, I was eventually labeled *The Lebanese Leprechaun* by Neal Shine, making me a qualified candidate for the inner city way of life. I could in no way fill the shoes of Fr. Kern — Nor could anyone else! — but I do believe, in at least some small measure, I became part of the downtown Runyan gang....

Also, *honorable mention* as Runyan characters may include Sr. Ann Currier, a street-smart Pastoral Minister who has worked more than two generations at Holy Trinity and Sr. Annette Zipple, a tireless and dedicated Social Worker for many years. With an overabundance of work to be done with those who passed through our doors each day, I must include, of course, Jerez Jackson. She was a knowledgeable, experienced, tough but very compassionate counselor who helped me maintain my sanity. She knew all the fine points of counseling in the inner city where there were rarely two cases alike. She was always in contact with other programs that were similar to the work at Holy Trinity or complimentary to our work. With her daily help, we kept up with the best counseling and service agencies. She was truly a special blessing to our Social Programs.

The succeeding Pastors: Frs. John Nowland, Tom Sutherland and Russ Kohler, (the present

Pastor of Holy Trinity) have all made their unique and personal contributions to the history of Holy Trinity.

Sr. Ann has covered every street in the neighborhood on foot, and knew every family personally, and more likely than not, helped all of them at one time or another. I was astonished at the amount of time she spent in the homes and in the hospitals caring for the sick, preparing them for the Pastor's role in performing the Anointing of the Sick and other Sacraments. We did this many times.

Sr. Ann was fearless. Some homes were thoroughly infested with vermin, roaches, mice and horrific odors. Nothing stopped her. I recall, on one occasion, she had several of us working on a single case. I will call her Madeline. Madeline was a character from a story book! She always wore a heavy overcoat and a hat with a wide brim whenever she walked over to the Parish House. She just lived one block away. It was quite surprising to see her practically wearing everything she owned. Even in the middle of the summer, during a

Fr. Jay anointing the sick

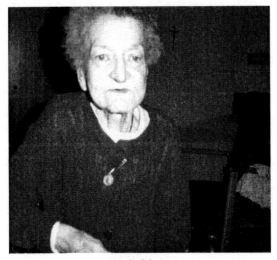

Madeline

heat wave, she would still be wearing her overcoat and hat.

When she became ill, everything changed. We did not see her for a long time. Sr. Ann informed us how terrible were her living conditions. She had us all working together cleaning out Madeline's apartment. What we witnessed was difficult to believe. The moment we opened her door, the odor practically made it impossible to breathe. It was necessary to hold our breath each time we entered. On our way out each time we would grab something to throw away. Apart from the odor, we were welcomed by a lot of living things. Roaches could be seen all over the table. Mice were running everywhere. They were apparently more afraid of us than we were of them. It took a long time to clear the room; we were eventually just throwing the mattress and other large objects out the window...to be picked up afterwards. I cannot describe the horrible condition of the mattress; I believe the center of it was totally corroded.

Sr. Ann took Madeline to the hospital for a number of health conditions she had. After a few days, I went to see her. She had the appearance of a totally new person in a clean, odorless, healthy environment. She was very excited about having everything in a spotless condition. However, at this point, she was closer to death than to life. At least her final days were lived with quality and care. Madeline made her transition in peace. We were all present at her funeral.

8. MEET SOME OF OUR PEOPLE

Who can map out the various forces at play in one soul? The hairs of his head are easier by far to count than his feelings and the movement of his heart.

-St. Augustine

THE CLERGY - Beginning in the nineteen-fifties, Fr. Kern was the Pastor and Fr. Raymond Schlinkert, the Associate Pastor. Msgr. Thomas Jobs, Director of the Propagation of Faith and Fr. Ignatius Duggan S.J., were in residence. Other priests residing at Holy Trinity were Fr. David Duncan, who was a former professor at Sacred Heart Seminary, Fr. Valentine Rodriguez who was originally from Spain and taught at Marygrove College and Fr. Verardi.

Most Holy Trinity Church and Rectory

Then, in the sixties, Frs. David Dillon, Leonard McManaman, Michael O'Neil and Hugh McDonald took up residence there. It was a big Rectory and it was always full.

Also, Residing at Holy Trinity at different times, were several other Hispanic priests visiting America for various reasons: some to learn English, others to acquire Degrees at one of our Universities and still others who were simply on vacation. A story could be told about each one. I knew most of them, but some were before my time. They all had a personal history that was captivating and colorful.

While in residence each of them would help if called upon but their service was minimal since they were actually not a part of the staff.

FR. EZEQUIEL MONDRAGON, directly from Toluca, Mexico, was a priest who came to help at Holy Trinity and also to learn English. We spent a lot of time working together, playing racquetball and sharpening his English and my Spanish. If Fr. Zeke also came here to learn about life, our clients were wonderful teachers because they were actually living what most of us just read or hear about: living on the street with no home, no car, no money, no bank accounts, no television, no radio, no closet with extra clothes, no extra pair of shoes and no food except what they line up to receive at a Soup Kitchen. The list of items we have and they do not is too long to include.

Fr. Zeke (a nickname for Ezequiel) told me in his own words: "I remember the day you (Fr. Jay) invited me to clean an apartment of a handicap lady who for a long time was confined to a wheelchair; I still have this unforgettable image of you and I entering that apartment with a terrible odor. The experience was eased because you taught me to clean the place with genuine love, straight from the heart. I then realized that Holy Trinity was open to every person in every kind of emergency situation. The conditions of the unfortunate didn't matter. They were our brothers and sisters."

Fr. Zeke goes on to say that one of the most touching things he remembered was lunch and dinner time, when people of different walks of life: doctors, lawyers, politicians, attorneys, nuns, priests and employees used to sit together at the table for a meal. However what they all had in common was their deep concern for the poor and how their lives were affected and changed by the very ones they were helping. Fr. Ezequiel is now an American citizen and is presently Pastor of Sacred Heart Parish in Imlay City, Michigan.

Holy Trinity kept its identity of welcoming those that nobody else wanted because the staff rarely distinguished between clients, such as *good ones or bad ones*. There were very, very few exceptions in my eleven years there. Everybody felt personally welcomed. That was underlying key that made Trinity famous.

Everyone who came through the doors of Holy Trinity walked away with a gift.

Yes, everyone received a gift, whether a handout or a handshake! They all walked away with something that can't be put into words.

* * * * *

Fr. DENNIS DILLON, S.J. God sent us every kind of personality. Some of the folks who came for help were quite unforgettable. I recall Jack Teller, one of the *Knights of the Road*. He was a rather tall fellow, thin for a couple of reasons: probably because of heredity and because of his many days on the streets. He was often unkempt-looking, especially in the colder season when he would sleep outside all night. Fr. Dennis Dillon, S.J., who helped with the Open Door Policy for nearly a year, worked with him on several occasions. He said it was easy to forget that he was actually a drifter walking the streets... particularly when Jack spoke. He had a deep, resonant voice, a quick mind, and a vast vocabulary, something like a has-been Shakespearean actor or John

Carradine from the films. He would keep
Fr. Dillon, myself or one of the staff members
into one of his many long conversations,
even after he discovered that his impressive
talks got him no more money than the usual
Trinity fifty cents or a dollar.

It was always a pleasure to talk with
him because he was so knowledgeable on many
different topics. Jack came from a good
family. One of his parents, he said, had
played with the Detroit Symphony Orchestra
and that he himself had gone to Harvard.
Fr. Dillon, taken by surprise, commented
that he happened to know someone who was
at Harvard at the very same time. When Jack
was quizzed a bit about Harvard, he easily
came up with enough information to make
a believer out of Fr. Dillon. Jack's sister
had her Doctorate in Psychology and was
a counselor in the Detroit Public School
System. This was verified after speaking
with his sister on a number of occasions.
We don't know how old Jack was but it was
clear that life on the streets was gradually
killing him. He had been through several
recovery programs but none of them worked
for him. He knew all the right answers,

but for him the way to get off the streets was not through the mind or right answers.

Somehow, he could never make a clean break. During the warmer months he would sleep in the open fields around Trinity so he would have more money for drink. In the winter, however, he began to feel the cold more and finally would sign his SSI check over to us so we could maintain a room for him in that single occupancy hotel across from the Michigan Central Train Station. We would also put some money on deposit at the little 'Greasy Spoon' on the hotel's first floor. So in winter, his happiness was mixed. His drinking bouts were limited, but he was at least warm and fed.

Fr. Dillon recalls: one winter day when I drove to the hotel to put down some money for his room, the manager, on receiving the money, said:

"This is for your brother, Jack." (Fr. Dillon was also tall and thin!)

"Yes," he said, and headed out the door to return to Holy Trinity. As Father walked with his head down, fighting the icy winds that swirled around the station, he knew why he liked Holy Trinity. It was a place where he could be treated like the people he served. He still has a pocket-sized , leather-bound, King James Version of the Bible which Jack gave him. In it is the memorial card from Jack's funeral. Jack died on the streets, still unable to do or be whatever would keep him alcohol-free.

Again, anyone working at Holy Trinity will agree that while taking care of the poor and homeless, we also learned great lessons. They actually taught us through their own struggles how to enable themselves to face life issues and I am sure their issues were much more challenging.

Christmas Pageant

Seder meal at Holy Trinity

SR. MARGARET HUGHES - Our Office staff and Volunteers were incredibly gifted and cooperative...all working together. One of the Sisters at the Convent of Holy Trinity, Sr. Margaret Hughes, I.H.M., was often included not only in school activities, but in general parish activities as well.

The Immaculate Heart of Mary Sisters living at Holy Trinity Convent also offered a helping hand. It was a different style of Ministry, but it was their contribution to the men and women who knocked at their back door seeking a portion of food. When they prepared dinner after school hours, they often made some peanut butter sandwiches for those who would come at meal time politely asking, "Sister, can you spare a pork chop," or they would proudly remind them, "I used to be an altar boy."

They settled for what they could get and always completed their request with a *thank you*. Sr. Marge, reflecting on those good ole days, said "In my thoughts while making the sandwiches and serving them, I recalled Jesus saying, "When I was hungry you gave me something to eat." We could also add, "There, but for grace of God, go I."

Each year on the Thursday before Easter, called Holy Thursday, we recalled Jesus having *the last supper* with His Apostles. It was also the Passover Meal, called the Seder Meal, reminding us of the hardship of the Jewish people during their Exodus from Egypt. We celebrated that traditional Seder Meal in our cafeteria. Annie Roland, of happy memory, along with the cafeteria crew, did the cooking. We had beef or lamb, along with the endive-bitter salad, apple salad, rive Jewish crackers and grape juice.

We expressed the traditional prayers, including: "Why is this Passover night so special?" We then listened to a reading from the Old Testament, particularly from the Book of Exodus. Then we added a reading from St. John's Gospel taken from the New Testament. The theme was *loving one another.* Everybody was invited: Parish and School Staff, parishioners, children, guests, personal friends and, as usual, our brothers and sisters who walked the streets.

There was always a sense of community, that we were all one and that we were all members of God's Family. This was truly a special night. Afterwards, we assembled in

Church for the washing of the feet and the celebration of the Mass, reminding us of the first Holy Thursday Eucharist solemnized by Jesus on the night before He died.

* * * * *

SISTER ANN CURRIER - The following was only one aspect of her kind of service. Sometimes the people we served turned out to be not who we thought they were. Surprises came often. Karen O'Meara was one of the ladies on the list for frequent visits because of ill health. She could not get out of bed...ever! Her body had lain in the same mattress for so many years that they were sort of inseparable. The deep impression in the middle of the bed was clear evidence. She had all the appearances of being extremely poor. She lived in a big old house near the Church — one of the early homesteads she inherited — and stayed for years in the same, exact corner room in the back. Sr. Ann visited her very often, sometimes every day.

Suddenly, everything changed. One day she discussed openly her background and a major event in her life. She even revealed an undisclosed and surprising secret; years ago she had *buried a treasure of cash* in the ground! She did this out of fear; she did not want anyone to know how much money she had...not even the banks. She continued her story, relating also that she went to the Holy Land in 1950. During that time, a change came over her. Upon her return, she dug up her money and kept it in the house. Sr. Ann convinced her to put her cash in a Deposit Box at a Federal Reserve Bank downtown Detroit. She did not immediately agree, but eventually she allowed Sr. Ann to take the money for her.

She asked if Sr. Ann believed in God. Her reply was "yes, of course!"

"Are you a thief?" She questioned further.

"No, I am not!" the nun affirmed.

I just want to be sure you are an honest person and not a thief. Those are my life's savings.

After gaining complete trust in the nun who had been voluntarily helping her for years, she agreed to have a will made out. Sr. Ann found a lawyer who would come to the house and set it up. When it was completed, the elderly lady promptly tore it up. Sr. Ann was disappointed and promptly told her to get her own lawyer. She did! It was the very same lawyer! Now, as for the money getting to a bank, that was another story. Incredible as it sounds, this same fearless Nun — in some mysterious manner, protected by God's Grace — *walked* from Most Holy Trinity Church about six long blocks in the inner city of Detroit to the Federal Reserve Bank, *carrying more than $100,000 in cash!*

When she got to the bank, she immediately asked to see the manager. They took her to a room and wanted to know what she had in mind. When she mentioned that she wanted to put $100,000 in the bank, they became suspect and she was instantly surrounded by guards. She said she wasn't sure whether the guards were for her protection or did they possibly think she was going to rob the bank!

"Where is the money you intend to deposit?" They asked cautiously, as they ushered her quietly to one of the cashier's windows.

"Right here!" She replied, as she opened her bag and began to place many thousand dollar bills and other large bills through a special cashier's window. The attendants' eyes popped out as they saw history being made before them. The manager openly professed that it was the largest deposit ever made in cash at their Federal Reserve Bank.

"What, exactly, do you want to do with this money?"

Sister responded that she wanted them to grant her ten certificates, each one worth $10,000. This was the will and desire of Miss O'Meara, who was thought to be a pauper. It was much easier to handle ten certificates than a large bag full of green American cash...and with each bill being a collector's item.

All of the above activities came at a time when Karen O'Meara's life span was growing short. The Will was made out as she finally brought everything out in the open. She had no living relatives that would inherit her fortune, so she gave it all to Most Holy Trinity Church, including several homes she also owned. She died peacefully and her funeral Mass, according to her request, took place at Holy Trinity. She had no idea what a blessing she was to the church. It just so happened at that time that the church was in a serious need of repairing the steeple. It became a hazard to anyone walking in the area of the church; loose pieces began to fall.

The Parish Staff prayed for some financial help to begin the repair work. Over $100,000 was needed. The response was quick and it came from the most unexpected source...a woman thought to be among the poorest in the neighborhood! Holy Trinity was always full of surprises and miracles! This was one of them. The elderly lady who was always receiving became a giver that day!

* * * * *

CHARLIE BULLETTE - Having good neighbors is important everywhere, especially in the inner city of Detroit. It was almost necessary to look out for each other. In Corktown, the area that includes Holy Trinity Parish, there were many folks walking the streets. In the seventies and eighties very few had cars; most were looking for help, a job or a meal. We had a God-send for a neighbor directly behind the church. Charlie was such a good friend, parishioner and neighbor. I had the privilege of conducting the funerals for Charlie's mother and his two brothers. They were originally from Switzerland and worked hard all their life.

When Charlie retired, he drove his mother to Belle Isle every day. He was a true care-giver. He also was a protector of Holy Trinity's buildings and property. Charlie walked around the church, the parish house and the school every night, making sure all was well. He knew the license numbers of the cars that parked in the area; a new vehicle was immediately identified by him and watched more carefully.

He also walked the streets every day — not as one of the Knights of the Road nor looking for a hand-out — but just to visit whoever was building a home, repairing property or simply to get some fresh air since and the church was not far from the Detroit River with its peaceful atmosphere. Going back in time, he was probably the oldest living member of Holy Trinity Church, being 93 years old when he was called to heaven. He and his brothers lived a very frugal and disciplined life. They cut each other's hair to save some money; they never re-decorated the house with new furniture or curtains and the floor was covered with simple rubber mats. Charlie even picked up a used newspaper from one of the benches at Belle Isle instead of having to purchase a paper every day.

Oddly though, Charlie was generous in other ways. He loved people and was very sociable. He helped make living among the homeless much more pleasant. He passed away not long ago; Charlie was a little guy who made a big impact on the lives of many...myself included! In my estimation, he was a true servant of God.

∗ ∗ ∗ ∗ ∗

VINCENT PRECA - Not every one who walked through our doors was looking for help. Another elderly man, named Vincent, attended church every day. Our daily Services began at 12:10 p.m. Vincent would arrive early and sit in the parish house for a while... after serving himself breakfast in the parish kitchen! We were happy that he made a daily appearance. Vincent was an interesting person. He wore a suit and tie every day and each morning he would appear with a fresh flower in his lapel. We never knew exactly where the flowers came from, but we had an idea that they were always in his path while walking to the church. Vincent looked and *actually was* quite fragile. He was small in stature and very thin, but his face was truly angelic with piercing eyes that emanated innocence.

One day, while walking in the neighborhood, Vincent got stuck in the mud. I mean that literally! He couldn't move; lacking strength and stamina, he stood there helpless. It just so happened that one of the Sisters was passing by. She did the only thing she could do. She untied his shoes and literally picked him up out of the mud. It was good

Sr Ann Currier

**Fr Jay giving Vincent
Preca a ride**

for a few laughs, but it could have turned into a serious situation had she not acted promptly.

Even the bus drivers knew this wonderful, innocent man. They would stop the bus right where he was slowly walking and pick him up, dropping him off a lot closer to where he was going.

Another time, Vincent was on his way to the Cadillac Nursing Home, but he wanted to stop at his *home* first. By home, he meant the parish house of Holy Trinity Church. He was given the Sacraments of the Sick. He gave the same response as he always did upon receiving Communion: I would say, "Vincent, the Body of Christ." He replied as usual, "With pleasure!"

Vincent's wife was not well and wanted to leave this life. She had given up after he died. She complained often that she would like to die and get away from it all; she was so unhappy and quite elderly, having the usual poor health that comes with age.

On one occasion she complained: "Why doesn't God just take me?"

"Why don't you listen to what God is saying to you?" Sister Ann replied.

The very next day, which was Good Friday, she passed away. Apparently, her sincere request was granted.

*   *   *   *   *

MAGGIE HAGGARD - There was a lady named Margaret Haggard who used to work around Trinity rectory counting the Sunday collection and doing other odd jobs. We all knew her well and were pleased that she spent most of her life helping us out in the Parish House. She became an honorary member of our Staff. Eventually, as her health deteriorated, arrangements were made for Maggie to go to the hospital, then to Carmel Hall; from Carmel Hall she was placed in

Kundig Center, and finally to the Cadillac Nursing Home.

Maggie died on September 10, 1985. When our angelic helper, Sr. Ann cleaned out Maggie's apartment, she found letters sent to her from her only son who was killed in service in 1945.

Morris Auger was his name. He was married and had a ten month old daughter named Frances whom he had never seen. Among Maggie's keepsakes were letters written by Frances, who discovered that her grandmother was the same Maggie we knew. She wrote often begging her grandmother to tell her about her father and sending her a picture of him. Sr. Ann never gave up easily. She tried to locate Frances for the last fourteen years, but every letter sent to several addresses all returned. Phone calls also failed to get results.

Joan Reagan, a receptionist and an active volunteer at Holy Trinity, was always successful in obtaining phone numbers. She took the basic information about Frances who was last heard from in Huntington, West Virginia. Frances last name would possibly be Auger or Plumons, with a son named Stewart.

Joanie made quite a few calls. She came up with a possible phone number. Sr. Ann followed up with phone calls until someone answered. It was Frances herself! They talked for hours that evening.

Maggie's personal items were sent to her granddaughter Frances, including a picture of her dad, letters written by the chaplain when her dad was killed in action and the small flag that her grandmother hung in her window. Also delivered to Frances were Maggie's Bible and the letters written to her mother. The newspaper from Bay City showed a picture of her dad on the front page and many more personal items, including one of her dad's report cards. What a joy it was to have the dream of a granddaughter fulfilled. Not all service at Holy Trinity is done on the spur of the moment. This one took fourteen years to complete! And without doubt, all the phone calls, letters and contacts made during that time easily made it worth while.

* * * * *

AND THEN THERE WERE THESE - Yet not everyone who came to the parish house was a blessing to us. Some were challenges! One of the men had a strange fetish when he entered. He would immediately go to the bathroom and come out after a considerable amount of time. After a few visits, we realized quite clearly what he was doing in there. He stuffed as much toilet paper as possible in the toilet bowl, making it impossible to flush. If there were a whole role of paper available, the entire contents would be shoved in as tightly as possible, sheet by sheet. One did not have to be a psychiatrist to realize that his actions were quite abnormal. Naturally, we had to bar him from ever using the bathroom again. We never liked having to restrict someone but he realized that he was making it difficult for those who also needed the restroom. They, on the other hand, expressed their anger quite openly over his eccentric behavior.

Then there was the man who always carried a suitcase when he walked in for assistance. In the beginning, we were unaware of what he had in those suitcases. We simply thought he was carrying all that he owned. That part was true, but he also came in the parish house with the intentions of loading up his suitcases! What I mean is that he would pick up anything that was not nailed or tied down as if they belonged to him. Not only books or magazines lying around but even valuables on the desk were not safe...if no one was looking! When he was finally caught with a bagful of goods, we did not allow him to enter unless he left the bags at the door outside.

THE BAPTISMAL REGISTRY was very helpful in finding one's roots in the Corktown area. The addresses recorded along with the reception of Baptism were sometimes the only link to one's past. Former parishioners would often ask if they could comb through our files to find a parent or a relative with whom all communication was gone.

Finding one's roots in today's world is very important to some families. Since the average American family consists of grandparents, who migrated here from various European, African or Hispanic countries, it is often difficult to know who one's ancestors are. Searching for the roots of Irish families, who once were parishioners of Holy Trinity, was quite easy. Usually, their parents were Irish on both sides. Our records were very specific and sometimes detailed. We enjoyed watching a couple get excited just observing their ancestors names in the Registry. It gave them a link to

their past and presented a larger picture
of their family structure.

9. MORE THAN JUST

COUNSELING

The worst sin toward our fellow creatures

is not to hate them,

but to be indifferent to them.

-George Bernard Shaw

JEREZ JACKSON - She helped raise the work at Holy Trinity to a new level. God gave me such a wonderful Staff to work with. Sometimes the image of Holy Trinity is that we just donated a little money to the people who came to our door. As we observed in Maggie's story, that is simply not true! Rather, counseling and assistance of every

Fr. Jay and Mrs. Jackson

kind was our daily work...and that took time!

Just to give a *handout* is only a *band aid* operation! Yes, we did that, but there was so much more to offer. Much of what we did was also a referral program that is, sending a person to another organization or location in order to receive help beyond our budget and our capacity.

Each of them had a story to tell, a problem to solve, a need to be filled. The needs were many: advice, counsel, money, clothes and toiletries, a hair cut, transportation, a driver's license, a place to stay, job listings, etc. There was no end to resolving each one's request. I was never prepared for this. I was 47 years old and had been assigned to seven other parishes in the Archdiocese of Detroit, but never was I faced with an *Open Door policy.*

If someone appeared at the door bleeding badly from a fight or a mugging, we didn't give a handout...we got that person to the emergency room at the hospital for immediate treatment. If they were present at the time when our medical clinic was open, we could send them across the street for immediate treatment by one of the volunteer doctors. If clothes were all one needed, especially in the winter, our Clothes Store would provide them with what they needed. Some folks came to us for counsel by an attorney. They would be given help by the volunteer lawyers who showed up in the evening each week.

Besides the food, clothing, and medical assistance, there were a number of people who were ready to move on in the educational field but were lacking funds. Mrs. Jerez Jackson was able to make an arrangement with Wayne County Community College for our clients to continue their education. One of our young men was able to get a Master's Degree in Engineering. About six others received their Bachelor of Arts Degrees and another half dozen got their Associate Degrees. Then there were some who needed their G.E.D. or equivalent to a High School Education. We were very pleased with the results. Those pursuing their accomplishments in education had a *life* they were building for the future. They would quickly be off the streets and become a formidable part of society.

Mrs. Jackson also worked with a Doctor at Ford Hospital. This wonderful Jewish Doctor would arrange for treatment often when it was difficult to get through the process of being accepted with proper insurance and identification. On one occasion, there was a woman who came to Holy Trinity for help and was in a critical condition because of a large tumor. This same Doctor managed to have her treated immediately thus saving her life. And there were others who received medical attention for serious conditions. Finding the right help for the right problem was the key!

Another time, one of the Knights of the Road and familiar to us, was in a coma at the hospital. He was not responding when they called him by name. Mrs. Jackson went to the hospital to visit. She saw that they were getting nowhere with him, so she gave them his nickname. When they yelled his nickname in his ear, he slowly began to respond, eventually coming out of his coma.

On a number of occasions, a couple would come in for financial help and end up discussing their relationship. After a few visits and feeling more confident to talk about it, they made plans to be married at Holy Trinity. With proper preparations, an astonishing number of street people made their way to the altar together.

SISTER ANNETTE ZIPPLE - Another wondrous Staff member. The Most Holy Trinity *Community Outreach Program* was another effective mode of serving the larger Community. As Director, Sister Annette Zipple, a Social Worker, found many challenges to her calling to be of service at Holy Trinity, as well as to Southwest Detroit. As a Religious of the Sacred Heart, she was able to put into practice the mission of her Religious Order of making God's love visible in the heart of the world. Her energies were combined with those of dedicated *VISTA* volunteers and social work students from metro Detroit Universities who worked with her.

The need for education in both the traditional and alternative models was also a primary concern for Mrs. Jackson as well as Sr. Annette. Sister focused more closely on viable ways to address the lack of access for women to post Secondary Education and the need for quality recreational centers for youth. Sr. Annette also pursued cultural and thematic Art Programs to enable both personal and social development of the women she was with in her Ministry. Throughout

122

Sr. Annette Zipple

Friends of the family

the three decades she served at Holy Trinity, Sister Annette experienced tremendous joy in her service flowing from the ongoing struggle to find the resources that were needed to address the various social issues.

After retirement, Sister Annette continued a more concentrated effort in two programs initiated at Holy Trinity; namely, the Southwest Detroit Education Empowerment Program (SWEEP), a collaboration of the Religious of the Sacred Heart with the Felician Sisters and Madonna University enabling materially poor women who live and work in the Southwest Community to begin their post secondary education in their own community.

As with the men, we can imagine the joy in the families of fourteen women who will graduate in May, 2004 with a Bachelors in Social Work and the joy of over 80 other women who now know that this is possible for them as well. Many of these students began their educational efforts in the Trinity Moms and Tots Program *Linking the Arts with Literacy* that continues to use the media of the Arts to overcome both language and cultural differences, so often a challenge that blocks their educational hopes.

Service gives expression to joy, both for the people who are served and for the one who walks with them, in the mutual giving and receiving that is always present in truly Christian Service.

10. THE SOUP KITCHEN

Only a life lived for others is a
life worthwhile.

-Albert Einstein

The most well-known Soup Kitchen in
the city of Detroit is the one operated
by the Capuchin monks of St. Bonaventure
Monastery at 1820 Mt. Elliott near Jefferson
on the east side of Detroit. Their Soup
Kitchen precedes most Soup Kitchens by many
years, going back to 1929 during the
Depression. Fr. Solanus Casey was, at one
time, in charge of the Capuchin Soup Kitchen
which now serves 2,500 meals each day to
the less fortunate. Fr. Solanus Casey, who
is well known for his work with the poor,
his holiness and also the thousands of people
he healed, is soon to be the only person
from Michigan and also the first American
born male to be canonized a Saint in the
Catholic Church.

The west side of the city was in serious need of similar assistance. Trinity's very first Soup Kitchen was located on Bagley Street between Trumbull and Eighth, in the shadow of Tiger Stadium. Inspired by Dorothy Day whom they met personally, Lou and Justine Murphy were in charge of this very first Soup Kitchen on the west side of Detroit. Unable to continue maintaining such a huge project, they had to turn the operation of the Soup Kitchen over to a Church which could adequately handle management, workers, volunteers...and the abundance of food.

In 1977, when I arrived at Holy Trinity, there was no Soup Kitchen in the area. They had just closed the one in the neighboring church of St. Boniface. They were doing as well as a Church can while running a Soup Kitchen, but problems arose and they had to close down. It is a very demanding task to operate a church and a Soup Kitchen at the same time — especially if you have a school with young children. Both would require full-time attention and *extreme caution.*

Nevertheless, the very first Soup Kitchen in Corktown began when my Associate, Fr. Sam, and I decided that we had better start looking for another place where those in need could have their next meal on a daily basis. We drove up and down Michigan Avenue, the main street on our side of town, looking for a vacant building that would serve our needs. We thought we had found a perfect place for the Soup Kitchen; it was a closed store front right on Michigan Avenue just down the street from the former Tiger Stadium. We checked it over very carefully and concluded that it was a perfect place to get our Soup Kitchen started. We quickly made a purchase of the abandoned store and sent the word out that we were providing meals for anyone in need.

From the very beginning, the Soup Kitchen served over one hundred-fifty people daily. Word travels fast on the street! I felt quite elated to have been a part of such

128

an enterprise. In fact, the very evening when the first meals were being served to a long line of hungry folks, Fr. Sam and I celebrated the immediate success of this project with a good meal ourselves. However, *success* in the inner city is such an elusive word.

One learns very quickly that in the core inner city of Detroit, we have to accept one of the rarest of all virtues. We called it the *Virtue of Failability*. It describes the positive effect of continually introducing new projects in an area where success and failure develop side by side. There is a continual demand for new projects to counter any new problems — which we never ran out of — nor did we always succeed. Failure only means: to try again and maybe this time it will work. Or we move to the proverbial "Plan B" or other efforts.

Shortly after, as we were moving right along with our newest project and welcoming larger numbers of street people each week, we were served with an Ordinance from city authorities. Business men on either side of the Soup Kitchen made some serious legal complaints in Court that we were ruining their business. Everyday, around meal time, the Knights of the Road would gather in front of the buildings lining up to be served. The business people maintained that their clients were being intimidated...many of them too frightened to return! That was probably true to a certain extent. At any rate, the city agreed after much discussion and we were served with an official injunction to close and move out by a particular date. This was a sad day for all of us, especially the ones walking the streets. We had not thought of that possibility beforehand.

We continued to believe in The Virtue of Failability which conveys the exact opposite of being discouraged! The high moral quality of such actions is still present and it is built on a trust that Divine Providence will not let you down.

After considering all possiblities for another location for the Soup Kitchen, our staff decided that finding a church that has the space would be ideal. Holy Trinity Church was not the proper environment for a Soup Kitchen, because we had children in Kindergarten up to the fourth grade. And the school was very active.

We carefully considered all the churches in the area. We found a church nearby in which the conditions were ideal. Across the street from Tiger Stadium, on the corner of Michigan and Trumbull was the beautiful church of St. Peter's Episcopal. Unfortunately, the Episcopal Bishop was about to close this church because, they had only eighteen parishioners at the time. It was, without question, too small to continue. The Pastor, Fr. Bob McDonald and I were friends and I felt comfortable visiting him soon after our staff meeting, to see if he was agreeable to house the Soup Kitchen. Our brief visit had a positive result. The unexpected offer sounded exciting to both of us. We felt the church would never be closed since it was serving the community in the most charitable way and we would have a Soup Kitchen that did not interfere with any local business. Behind the church, there was a door that led to a large basement. That was perfect for our purposes. And there was no one to complain!

Not only did this course of action save the church, but their parish enrollment also grew in numbers by being more involved with indigent families. St. Peter's Church began to house some families in the Parish House and became more and more involved in community projects. The church soon became, as they say, *alive and well!* And so was our Soup Kitchen!

It wasn't all that easy. Having the right people serving people is also very important. It is not just another service. Two qualities were required: making a *commitment* and being *dedicated*. Where do you find such people? We did not have to look far. Just down the street on Trumbull Avenue was the Dorothy Day House, an organization following her principles of caring for the under-privileged. From the start, we needed a staff of workers to manage the Soup Kitchen. They ran the first short-lived Soup Kitchen forced into closure by local businessmen and were willing to manage the one in the basement of St. Peter's. They were not easily discouraged either. They were delighted to run a place where people could be fed.

It was in perfect keeping with the principles of Dorothy Day. I have been a great admirer of Dorothy Day since I first heard of her wonderful accomplishments fighting for the voiceless people who cried out for help. She was even jailed several times for civil disobedience facing challenges in favor of our poorer brothers and sisters.

Dorothy Day had led an unusually eventful life. She was born in 1897 in Brooklyn Heights, New York, the third child of Christian parents. They did not, however, practice their faith. She was baptized Episcopalian at the age of 12, but put religion aside in her later teens and joined the Socialist Party. She became involved in civil disobedience and was jailed more than once. Later, in December of 1927 she became a member of the Roman Catholic Church, continuing her efforts to defend the rights of others. Her fondest desire was to care for and feed those who had no place to call their own. She opened her first House of Hospitality and produced the first Catholic Worker newspaper in 1933 along with Peter Maurin, who inspired her deeply.

Jim Forest writes in his *Biography of Dorothy Day*, "Among those who came to visit her when she was no longer able to travel was Mother Teresa of Calcutta, who had once pinned on Day's dress the cross worn only by fully professed members of the Missionary Sisters of Charity. Long before her death, November 29, 1980, Day found herself regarded by many as a saint. No words of hers are better known than her brusque response, "Don't call me a saint. I don't want to be dismissed so easily." Nonetheless, having herself treasured the memory and witness of many saints, she is a candidate for inclusion in the Calendar of Saints. The Claretians have launched an effort to have her canonized."

"If I have achieved anything in my life," she once remarked, "it is because I have not been embarrassed to talk about God." Shortly after her passing, we had a Memorial Mass in her honor at Holy Trinity. I am sure there were many prayers of admiration and gratitude offered for her in the areas where she touched so many lives.

Today there are over 130 Catholic Worker Communities in thirty-two States and eight foreign countries. One of them is the Dorothy Day House on Trumbull Avenue in Detroit near Holy Trinity Church! We were fortunate to have such a Community so close. Fr. Tom Lumpkin, Peter Weber and Mary West took on the responsibility for getting us started again with a Soup Kitchen that is still in operation after 25 years. Today, over 500 meals are served every day. And Holy Trinity and St. Peter Church still are Sponsors for the Soup Kitchen and meet several times each year concerning its needs and future.

11. PARISH COMMUNITY COUNCIL

We have always known that heedless self-interest was bad morals; we know now that is bad economics.

-Franklin D. Roosevelt

Parish Councils came into existence after the Vatican II Council. They were designed to represent the total parish community and assist the Pastor in an advisory capacity. Each parish had its own way of designating members on the Parish Council. It was usually done by offering the parishioners at large to vote for the candidates of their choice. Besides the five (or seven) voted at large, four commissioners representing Worship, Christian

Service, Administration, and Education were also added to form the Parish Council. These four Commissions cover most of the activities of an ordinary parish.

We, in the inner city, had to make a slight adjustment in our arrangement. Working with individuals and families who walked the streets or who were always in financial trouble and who moved in and out of the whole inner city area, demanded by its very nature...*a shared action*. There were so many overlapping activities by so many organizations and churches of various denominations that it naturally followed to have all the congregations and groups included at our parish council meetings — not every meeting — but often.

Besides the members of Holy Trinity Parish present, including representatives from the Mexican, Puerto Rican, Maltese and Irish communities, I welcomed representatives from Day House who served the Manna Community Soup Kitchen, St. Peter Episcopal and Fort Street Presbyterian, which opened its doors once a week to offer a shower, a change of clothes and a meal to anyone in need; the Farm Workers Union, forever fighting for the rights of their Migrant workers; Alternatives for Girls; C.O.T.S., which provided lodging for families; Dignity, a gay community which celebrated Mass each week at Holy Trinity Church; the Salvation Army Rescue Mission and Kelly's Rescue Mission. And still others at various times.

We all had a common purpose: building up the Family of God by serving our brothers and sisters who needed our assistance. Without the presence of the needy and homeless, many of the organizations would not exist.

We were an awesome gathering, comprised of leaders representing the most dedicated churches or organizations in the area. We had no trouble working together because we did not dwell on our differences. There was work to be done! We all had projects that we envisioned for the people we served. *When one's ministry is in the inner city, teamwork is the key to success.* Holy Trinity's service to the community was probably more well known than the others since we had frequent coverage on television, radio and the newspapers. So it was quite appropriate to have the meetings at Holy Trinity. And the name given was *The Holy Trinity Community Council.*

We accomplished a lot together. We could refer our clients to the appropriate organization that performed special services. If a girl showed up who was pregnant and out on the street, we would immediately contact *Alternatives for Girls*; if a woman with children came into town and had no place to stay, we would refer them to C.O.T.S. If they needed a shower or change of clothes, Fort Street Presbyterian welcomed them. We all had a gift to offer, depending on the circumstances.

By knowing one another personally, we felt no barriers that made us feel uncomfortable in seeking help from one another. I never in my heart thought that one group's service was better than another. In my view, we were all equally putting out a combined effort to bring the peace of God to those whom God sent to us.

I also learned that my personal belief system as a Roman Catholic priest was not the most important factor in our combined efforts. It was the openness, the flexibility, the cooperation and the proper motives of service that made our projects become realities.

Besides all of the above, Holy Trinity's Parish Council continued to focus on the spiritual and material guidance of our own parishioners and those who knocked on our door for help. Leadership and direction for our own people remained the primary effort. In the pre-Vatican days, most churches only cared for their own concerns, without much regard for the other parish communities. By its very nature, Holy Trinity was an exception! Even before the church could be used as a place of worship, it became the first hospital in the Detroit area. The cholera epidemic of 1834 ravaged the

141

city and Holy Trinity was positioned in the heart of the city, a perfect setting for a hospital.

Since the first pastor of Holy Trinity was also the city's Administrator for the Poor, a forerunner for the welfare system, those living at poverty level were served from the very beginning regardless of where they lived. Since then, however, each successive Pastor at Holy Trinity maintained a love of service to the whole community. In Fr. Kern's time, such outstanding service reached the attention of the entire Metropolitan Detroit area and beyond through the public media.

12. SAVING THE NEIGHBORHOOD

*There is no such thing as justice -
in or out of court.*

-Clarence Darrow

*One hour of justice is worth a
hundred of prayer.*

-Arab Proverb

SHIRLEY BEAUPRE was a faithful parishioner of Holy Trinity, who cared deeply about the Parish Community and the Corktown neighborhood. She was and still is, a doer. Talking was fine, but as one dedicated, she was always ready to see a project through, regardless of the sacrifice of time and

143

energy involved. She lived near the Church and was very much a part of the Parish Family.

Back in the seventies, a Basilian priest from St. Anne's Parish, located about a mile away, gave a talk at Holy Trinity on what was then called: Liberation Theology. He focused on the death and resurrection of a Parish Family. He encouraged all present to draw attention to the biggest death signs in Corktown, where the greatest liberation was needed.

One sign included the two vacant blocks in the heart of the Parish, an obvious eyesore. To resolve the problem by building new family homes in that area, a Housing Committee was formed. It was called the Holy Trinity Non-Profit Housing Corporation (HTNPH). Those who initially incorporated the HTNPH were John Lansing, Mr. Rojas, and Shirley Beaupre. They met regularly, for about a year, with attorneys and architects, seeking ways to finance and develop housing in the vacant area. They planned well and did their homework, but unfortunately, the area selected was refused assistance by the city planners.

Peter Tavarez, Jessie Mifsud and Shirley Beaupre surveyed another area south of Michigan Avenue. At the same time, President Nixon opened up some federal money for neighborhood housing. With the assistance of Bill Warden, a long time friend of Holy Trinity and brilliant in matters of Historic Designation and Neighborhood Development, a major strategy was designed. This resulted in creating ten different organizations under the umbrella corporation HTNPH. Each organization had a piece of work to research. They were coached by Fr. Kern for their public speeches and, at his request, asked that a city planner be assigned to Corktown.

Having a city planner sit with the Coalition Team was a distinct advantage among the thousands of block clubs throughout the city of Detroit. Still, only 20 Urban Renewal Groups got funded. In response, six groups met and formed the Detroit Block Grant Coalition, studying why such a small fraction of the city got funds for continuing Urban Renewal and a vast area of the city got nothing. The City Council was shocked! This got the attention of Councilwoman Erma Henderson who assigned Sarah Foley, her staff person, to study the Coalition's request.

When the smoke cleared after four rounds of public hearings, a new category of funding non-urban renewal neighborhood groups was created, called The Neighborhood Opportunity Fund (N.O.F.)

The six groups that previously met all received funds. Sufficient financial help was given to rehabilitate five homes in Corktown. It was a beginning! What happened at Holy Trinity gave hope to about 200 groups each year that do get funding. This is Liberation Theology in action. People who care, people who group together to form a strong base. Fr. Kern always spoke of what he called *people power*. I found that to be true in my Ministry following Fr. Kern. The few in power are usually overwhelmed by the power that resides in the people they serve. We can add that bit of information to our theme of "in service is found happiness." Action, power and liberation also are results of people united in their service of others.

Another general situation surfaced around the same time. José Moncivais, with additional children, wanted to buy Jessie Mifsud's house to obtain more space. Jessie was more than willing to sell with intentions of moving to California. José Moncivais, however, was not able to get an $8,000 loan from any bank in the area. It was their policy not to lend mortgage money under $15,000. He appealed to the Holy Trinity Non-Profit Housing Corp. who studied the matter seriously. After attending a Chicago Conference that included the issue of Bank Loans, they became aware of a policy among banks known as *redlining*...in which loans were refused to the poorer classes.

This was brought to the attention of the City Council of Detroit. Again, Erma Henderson, along with Shirley Beaupre and

Miss Hertha enlightened the City Council about the serious problem of redlining. It was not a Detroit problem only; it was a national problem. I had been aware of redlining before I came to Holy Trinity. When I was a member of the Pontiac Ecumenical Ministry, composed of clergy persons, we were fighting redlining there as well. It was a battle still going on.

Beverly Manic of Detroit's Michigan Avenue Community Organization (MACO), carefully collected banking information about MACO residents banking deposits. She discovered that one bank alone received deposits of $52 million from that neighborhood. *But there was not one person who could get a mortgage loan from that bank!* She charted this sort of banking information graphically for her presentations. It was very effective. Mrs. Erma Henderson established an Anti-Redlining Committee which received state-wide attention. This led to the passage of State Law #135 known as the Community Reinvestment Act, which requires banks to reinvest in the neighborhoods where they are located. It later reached national attention and federal laws were imposed.

As a result of this whole incident, the banks are much more cooperative. Jose got his $8,000, the Corktown Consumer Housing Coop received $5,000 and later, $15,000. The CCHC even partnered with banks to build low/moderate income family housing. In fact, over fifty percent of all the new housing being built in the city of Detroit is by such small neighborhood groups, working cooperatively with the banking industry. Holy Trinity, once again, with helpers like Shirley Beaupre and Erma Henderson, led the way for a deeper sense of freedom through service and sacrifice.

13. EDUCATING CHILDREN

OF

MULTI-CULTURAL FAMILIES

A discussion arose among the disciples as to which of them was the greatest. Jesus, Who knew their thoughts, took a little child and placed it beside Him, after which He said to them, "Whoever welcomes this little child on my account welcomes me, and whoever welcomes me welcomes Him Who sent me; for the least one among you is the greatest."

-Luke 9: 47,48

The history of Holy Trinity is also, in part, a history of Detroit. Although the School System in Detroit is still not operating on an ideal level of education,

Former Holy Trinity School

there have been enormous improvements through the years. Holy Trinity School, at one time, represented the worst conditions imaginable. On August 16, 1957, nine Sisters, belonging to the Immaculate Heart of Mary Religious Community, and skilled in teaching, arrived at Most Holy Trinity School.

In the early years Holy Trinity School was a large building with its four floors fully occupied. On the first floor was the St. Frances Cabrini Medical Clinic and Reception Room. The Clinic was staffed by volunteer Doctors from Ford Hospital. On the same floor were the cafeteria and kitchen, as well as the Principal's Office and the Friends of the Family Center. Only two lavatories served the entire building...both located on the first floor. This was not a comfortable situation!

Grades one through eight occupied the second and third floors while the Kindergarten children used the Auditorium on the fourth floor for an hour's rest. The Auditorium was also utilized for occasional performances for the Parish Community.

Trinity School was anything but adequate. The desks were in very poor condition. They had so many grooves, markings and engravings on them that the children had difficulty writing on them. Tuition was five dollars but the children were told not to worry about tuition payments or school supplies. The children were given sufficient paper for writing, but the paper came from students of another school who had previously written on one side of each sheet. In other words, it was *used material* that was handed out to the children at Holy Trinity School.

Even the pencils and other supplies were provided by other schools because Trinity

School could not afford them nor could the parish provide the necessary funding to purchase them. Much later, new crayons, pencils and *unused* blank sheets of paper were finally provided for the children. This was a giant step in progress!

Sr. Ann Currier was one of the teachers. She reminded me that in those days, the only limit for the number of students in a classroom was the number of seats available. Coupled with that situation was the problem of having children of migrant and immigrant families who spoke no English. Incredibly, she was given the responsibility of teaching eighty-two students. By today's standards that would constitute about three classrooms of students just speaking English!

The Sisters at the school attempted to enroll children in advance for the oncoming year. However, according to Sister Frances Chireo and Sister Mary Pierce, it was difficult to enroll in advance, because many of the children would not show up. They couldn't! The families were migrant workers. They followed the seasons: picking cherries, pickles, sugar beets, cotton and tomatoes. Maybe by December, the children would arrive at school. They were the poorest of the poor. What they had on was all they owned! Because of their large families, the School Staff strongly believed in getting the children out of their homes with a full day of kindergarten. What developed was *the first all-day Kindergarten Program.* Part of the purpose of having such a Kindergarten Program was to give the mothers of larger families a little rest, too.

The majority of these Mexican migrant families ended up in Detroit because of the booming automobile industry. Holy Trinity Parish was able to get the men a steady job working on the assembly line in one of the big-three factories. Other nationalities in the Parish included Puerto Ricans, Maltese, Irish, Lebanese, African Americans, Native Americans and a smattering of others.

Holy Trinity School always operated in the red. The government gave the school two cents per meal, making it impossible to buy proper nourishment for the students. The I.H.M. Sisters, once again, were the greatest benefactors. Teaching children who were very hungry or starving did not work, so their Motherhouse in Monroe provided

154

a healthy lunch program for both the Convent and the school, supplying them with potatoes, eggs, turkey meat, vegetables, and bread. Lou Murphy, being in charge of the Corktown Coop. Kitchen, also provided some of the above.

During the winter season, Carmen, the school cook, would have hot chocolate for the children as they arrived. Quite often, because of frozen pipes at home, even the mothers would come to the school to keep warm. The babies would be taken care of in what was called the *Family Room*, while the parents found a warm spot in the school corridor.

A few more shocking statistics about Holy Trinity School: only $11.00 per child came in for tuition and supplies. And yet, school began with about four hundred children. By Christmas, the enrollment increased to four hundred and fifty. It was not unusual to have seventy-five or eighty kindergarten children in one classroom. Still, there were only twenty-three desks.

Some tables and chairs were found in the church, school and rectory basement.

They served a good purpose after a much-needed, severe scrubbing before being placed in a classroom.

The children, of course, learned English very quickly. The twenty-five or thirty children in kindergarten each year, who only spoke a foreign tongue, were fluent in English by December. They were then able to speak and interpret for their parents as well.

SISTER MAURA was principal of the school before I arrived at Holy Trinity. Her reputation was bigger than life! She had spent her prior teaching years with the poor. She believed that God gives gifts to all, the rich and the poor. She also supported, encouraged, and pushed teachers to do their best. Sister Maura begged, borrowed and did whatever was necessary to get furniture, writing equipment, and books for the school. Along with a Staff of dedicated teachers, Sr. Maura, left the school in excellent condition after six years of a truly committed service. New books, furniture, supplies, and a library were all available to Sr. Paula Marie, who followed her as principal. Then, during my eleven years as Pastor, the principal, Sr. Irene Therese, I.H.M., continued the legacy of providing the right atmosphere for learning and offered an encouraging curriculum for the students to blossom and excel in their studies.

Having taken over the responsibility of washing dishes in the Cafeteria, the Sisters trained the young people to follow directions and how to work in cooperation. They later found jobs for them at fast-food restaurants and Frank's Nurseries.

14. THE PERSONALITY

OF A PARISH

When a man dies,

he clutches in his hands only

that which he has given

away during his lifetime.

-Jean Jacques Rousseau

Like people, every parish, church or
religious community has a distinct personality.
There are parishes with outstanding choirs
dressed in exquisite garments. These
magnificent choirs add much to the services
which may appear, at times, to be quite
dull without their angelic voices. In fact,
in some churches, the choir is the main
event, inspiring souls to a new level of

worship and praise...along with Word of God proclaimed through their presiding Minister.

Some churches concentrate on their schools, which are very active and demand more attention than any other aspect of parish life. There is not only the image to maintain in the total community, but there are usually budgets that have to be met. Often, the church helps the school to remain in existence with a limited percentage of funds permitted through Diocesan Policy. There is always a struggle to make ends meet, because Catholic Schools operate independently of the City and State School Offices.

It is not unusual to witness a school barely surviving. The increasing expenditures often offset a limited budget. There is much energy and commitment necessary to make a school viable in some areas. Other schools with a large enrollment and an attractive location do extremely well. Nevertheless, a strong commitment is needed regardless of how dedicated a parish may be. The focus remains the same: upkeep and support for the school is of paramount importance.

Parishes without a school draw a different picture. They spend a great deal of energy in building up elaborate Religious Education Programs for the children of parishioners who attend public school. Under such conditions, Religious Education is the principal focus since those young students will constitute an important role in the future of that parish.

Finally, there is the inner-city parish such as Holy Trinity, which could best be described as a huge Christian Service Program. Holy Trinity was indeed unique! Holy Trinity was the gate...and I was plunged into the role of gatekeeper of an unknown number of nameless people. Unlike any other church community I ever witnessed or served, Holy Trinity was operating on a spiritual dimension high above an ordinary parish center of Christian Service.

The principal work at Holy Trinity was serving the whole community and establishing Outreach Programs. One of the main programs at Holy Trinity was the Open Door Policy in which many thousands of persons came through our doors every year. Observing the several cabinets filled with documented records of every person assisted, including the records of the Medical and Legal Clinic, gives clear evidence of helping more than 30,000 people each year. Holy Trinity became synonymous with *Open Door Policy*; for this, it was well known by the media. Ample coverage of the Open Door policy was given by the newspapers, television and radio stations.

One of the main reasons for such a successful program was that everything we did was also in the open. Donations came in every day, but so did the services to the less fortunate. Anyone passing by the church could visibly *see their donations in action every day*. Money came in one hand and went out the other. There was a deep sense of trust between giver and receiver.

It is quite remarkable that every time we needed financial assistance, it was there! We never doubted that God would abandon such programs that would help the least of his sons and daughters. Donations came in various forms, the bigger ones in the most unpredictable ways. Anyone who believes that only the priests are the ones to be honored in an inner city parish is badly mistaken.

Sometimes, at Holy Trinity, honor was given to those we served. I recall on one occasion, a Christmas tree was placed in my office. The desk was moved aside, allowing several Knights of the Road to sleep around the tree for the night. One of our Staff members, Frank, also gave them a pillow and a blanket. This was not an ordinary Christmas eve in a Parish House, nor was it an ordinary Christmas eve for our brothers from the street. It was a holy moment. It was a Holy Night!

Without the cooperation and generosity of parishioners, the many thousands of families in Michigan and out-State areas who made weekly donations for support, the wide-spread coverage of the good work being done and proclaimed by the various forms of news media, the prayers of many and the daily encouraging letters...all of these set up a fail-safe program to assist the poorer members of God's Family.

15. THE MANY FACES OF

TRINITY

One man with God

is always in the majority.

-John Knox

Since Holy Trinity began nearly 170 years ago, there were many stages of growth and expansion it experienced. From the early Eighteenth Century to 1977 when I arrived, there was a mountain of history that had accumulated as part of Trinity's Family life. I will not include every organization that was still present when I became Pastor, but I know there were at least 30 different societies or organizations in the parish. I call these the faces of

Trinity. The following are only samples of the many others too many to name.

THE ST. FRANCES CABRINI MEDICAL CLINIC. There are various forms of service maintained by volunteer Doctors from Henry Ford and Providence Hospital. Besides their own practice, they come down into the inner city and give free examinations, prescribe medications and send a patient to an appropriate Doctor or Hospital should there be a need for further assistance. Most often, they handle the average patient immediately. Volunteer parishioners also emerged as helpers at the Clinic. They, too, were another surprise blessing.

The Clinic was truly a gift for the many folks living in Corktown and the surrounding area. Without any insurance, they received medical help from professional Doctors, who added dedication and love for the poor to their unique services. The Medical Clinic was founded by Eugene Payne, Doctor Malcolm and Fr. Kern, and was open, originally, during the school hours five days a week.

If there were any need for medical assistance, Mary Matron, the Clinic Director and a volunteer, was there to assist. Mary Medrano took charge of the clinic two nights each week.

Miss Eileen Troester followed Mary Matron as director of the Medical Clinic until her deserved retirement after 25 years of dedicated service to the people in the area. St. Frances Cabrini Medical Clinic is still going strong, having celebrated its 50th anniversary in the year 2000.

Times have changed and so have the procedure for handling the clients at the Clinic. There are now about 41 million Americans who are uninsured. More than a hundred adults and children come to Trinity's Clinic every week, receiving free services for everything from a simple ear infection to mental health counseling, home health supplies and prescription assistance. Many of the patients are unable to purchase medications to control even common conditions such as hypertension, diabetes and heart disease. Tragically, some of them have Crohn's disease and Lupus; others are kidney-transplant patients who need anti-rejection drugs.

Are all of the above people without jobs? Not at all. Eight out of ten uninsured people *have* jobs. Sr. Mary Ellen Howard, a member of the Religious Sisters of Mercy, has been Director of the Cabrini Clinic since 1995. She has adequately handled the operational aspect of the Medical Clinic with superior results, even moving the Clinic to a new level of service several times since then. She has many sad stories to tell. One of them is about a young man who called her recently. He said:

"I am a truck driver, and I have a hernia so painful that I can't drive. The doctor at first told me I needed surgery right away. When he found out that I had no health insurance, he left the room and returned with a list of clinics where I could go. He said, maybe I didn't need the surgery after all. Now I'm in constant pain. I lost my job and my apartment. I am homeless.

I can work and I want to work. I want to drive. Can you help?"

His question is larger than life with resounding echos throughout all of our American Society. When will our government awaken to the responsibility of taking action on such an important key domestic issue facing our country? Basic health care is a *right*, not a *privilege* for only those who can afford it!

The St. Frances Cabrini Clinic which started at Holy Trinity in 1950, is the oldest free Clinic in the United States. It has served many thousands of uninsured working families since then. The Clinic continues to grow with the needs it encounters. It is staffed by over eighty volunteer physicians, physician assistants, nurses, nurse practitioners, pharmacists, and other health care professionals.

Even though fifty-nine percent of Detroit's population have an income below the federal poverty level and over 280,000 persons are

Fr. Jay with Dr. and Mrs. Djiuba

uninsured in Wayne County, twenty primary care clinics have closed in Detroit since 1998! So does it come as a surprise that Detroit ranks #1 among 687 cities across the country where hospitalization could have been prevented or avoided for those between 40 and 64 years of age?

The Cabrini Clinic of Holy Trinity Church is more important than ever with Health Status measures for Detroit being much worse than the state average, including: hospitalizations for asthma, infant mortality, incidence of HIV, Hepatitis B, late stage prostate cancer, invasive cervical cancer and late stage breast cancer.

We are not the only ones proud of the Cabrini Clinic. The Clinic has received many Awards, including the United Way Community Service's *Heugli Award for Program Excellence*, Pfizer Pharmaceutical's *Quality of Care* Award, the voices of Detroit Initiative *Champion for the Underserved* Award and the RARE Foundation's *Health Care* Award.

* * * * *

THE LEGAL CLINIC - Companion to the Medical Clinic was and still is the Legal Clinic in which lawyers come voluntarily to serve those who could not afford to hire an attorney. And there were many! These dedicated men and women work a full day and then come to serve others freely. Serving and giving of one's talents and time is its own reward, just as love is its own reward.

We were very proud of all our volunteers. The attorneys come on Thursday evenings and there are always those who have an old or new problem that needs professional help.

During my years as Pastor of Holy Trinity, I always looked forward to Thursday evenings. We had supper with the attorneys assigned that particular evening and our discussions were always amusing and enlightening. We fed them since they came right from work. With renewed energy that comes from bringing joy and help to others, they began their work.

They were confronted with every kind of problem: custody of the children, divorce proceedings, domestic violence, Probate Court, Deeds for property, and occasionally, criminal activity. There were many Hispanic families having difficulties with Immigration; a Spanish-speaking lawyer was needed in some cases, which we provided when necessary.

We were fortunate to have someone organize the schedule for the attorneys. Becky Tavarozzi, taking over from Mary Turner — who was hired by an Hispanic Organization which we will refer to later on in this book — fulfilled this role. Mrs. Tavarozzi was not an attorney, but she had the skills and the patience to make sure the attorneys were kept informed concerning their scheduled time and day of serving the public. There are about 20 attorneys now available, but that was not always so.

There was a time when the lawyers were very few. I recall, during my tenure at Holy Trinity, Judge Joe A. Sullivan and Judge Tom Brennan left their benches at court to take care of clients at Holy Trinity. No jury and no sentences! Just serving people! All the lawyers were gifted and knew how to help the simple folks who, in many cases, did not know their civil rights or proper procedure when dealing with the Law. Paul Manion, Seymour Berger and Brian Sullivan, now a Judge of the Circuit Court, were also part of this great team.

At the lowest point in its history of having enough lawyers to take care of the Legal Clinic properly, we are very grateful to Judge Gail McKnight who put the word out to a group of Irish Attorneys and got marvelous results. At least ten signed up. The Legal Clinic continues and its service cannot be measured in terms of results and percentages. Each case is of vital importance to someone who is fighting to have custody of a child or is running to find a place of escape from an abusive marriage, or who is about to be evicted in the middle of winter in freezing temperatures.

God bless these noble men who value the life of others beyond any cost or repayment! I am sure their hearts are filled with happiness as their work of service lives on.

THE FRIENDS OF THE FAMILY were also located in the school building. In charge was Lucy Estrada and other very dedicated ladies: Mary Louise Bell, Joan Mendoza, Theresa Robinson, and Mrs. Stimpson. They had many helpers. They did not just wait

174

for people to come to them and assist them in a brief encounter with their problems. Rather, these ladies were rare doers! They would go into the homes of people who come from a different culture and background.

Some of the women visited needed to be taught basic things: showing them how to care for each room in the house, how to clean, and how to do the wash. It may sound strange to us that some women actually did not know how to use a washing machine. After showing the families proper housekeeping, ladies from the Friends of the Family, under the direction of Sr. Annette Zipple, would follow up with a weekly visit, then move on to the next home. Their group was established to serve!

They even showed mothers how to make layettes and clothes for babies and how to get assistance. They were taught the power of cooperation. Families that were poor would bring in food three times a week from their homes. Learning new skills in the preparation of foods, they discovered that, together, there was more than sufficient food for themselves and other families...whereas individually they did not have enough food. Eventually, additional food was achieved through government surplus.

Many of the families shopped at the Salvation Army store on Lafayette and Sixth. That was as far as they ever went since the majority of them did not own a car. (Now, only a parking lot remains there since the Salvation Army later moved to Fort Street.)

*   *   *   *   *

THE HOLY TRINITY CORKTOWN COOP was composed of men who were striving to stay 'on the wagon' and, like the St. Vincent de Paul Society, would go and pick up used furniture and clothing. In the coop store, the men sold donated goods at a price that the poverty-stricken families could afford. In the event that they were unable to pay even the smallest amount, our men just simply gave families whatever they needed. The reason they asked for money in the first place was to give them a sense of dignity that they actually purchased those goods. Many of them walked out with a sense of pride.

Surprisingly, with the arrangement of selling the clothes, furniture, lamps, appliances, etc. in the Coop Store at the lowest possible price, the Coop provided a sizable, financial contribution to Holy Trinity.

The last coop store was located on Michigan between Trumbull and Eighth Street and run by Frank Murphy. It remained open for several years until a fire destroyed the store and its contents.

The need for used clothing and furniture was still at a high. Used clothing was dropped off at the Parish House where some basic clothing was given to those needing immediate help. The rest was picked up by the St. Vincent de Paul Society. Later, we simply made out referral slips for clothing assistance at the St. Vincent de Paul Stores.

* * * * *

FOUR LEAF CLOVER CLUB - Another servant of God, Helen Wagner, took over programs for Senior Citizens. She had them coming in from several parishes surrounding Holy Trinity Church. She was a great lady, spending her energies on taking care of the elderly. The Club was established to keep the Seniors active and to maintain friendship with other Seniors, who, at that time were a neglected part of Society.

Once a month, lunch would be served followed by Bingo and other games. Between two hundred and two hundred and fifty Seniors attended each month. Besides making all the preparations, Helen and the other ladies belonging to the Four Leaf Clover Club also had a follow-up system to remind some of the Seniors to attend each month... especially those in particular who tended to forget.

*   *   *   *   *

THE ST. JUDE SOCIETY also was quite active during my Pastorate. The members were recovering alcoholics who came from the Detroit Metro area. Well over one hundred attended Mass on the first Sunday of the month. After Mass they were served breakfast in the school cafeteria, followed by their monthly meeting.

The first time I had Mass and breakfast with them, I stood in front of the microphone to offer a prayer and a talk. Then, I made a statement they did not hear often. The talk was usually given by someone who had been through their programs for recovering alcoholics and the first thing they would declare was, "I am an alcoholic," then they would proceed with their talk. My first words were, "I am not an alcoholic." Those words alone separated me from the comradery and solidarity they had with each other. I believe I gave a talk that was interesting and appropriate, but in my heart I knew that I could not experience a certain joy and bonding they had with each other. Again, Holy Trinity was a beacon of light and service to a particular group.

* * * * *

ST. THOMAS AQUINAS READING ROOM - Holy Trinity is best known for its Open Door Policy, but before its enormous popularity of helping many thousands each year, there were other services that were cut short. Fr. Kern opened up a room called the *St. Thomas Aquinas Reading Room* located on Third Street in what was called *China Town*.

Anyone could just walk in off the street. They would get out of the cold, take a shower, sit, read, and enjoy the day. The St. Thomas Aquinas Reading Room did not remain open because of a familiar opposition — the same as before: the complaints from neighboring business men. They, too, claimed that their business was seriously impaired.

Sometime later, there were near-by buildings that were converted into dormitory-style rooms large enough to house many beds. At that time, it only took ten cents for a man to have a place to sleep for the night.

They needed, however, to come up with the money. Msgr. Jobs was in residence at the time, and he would hand out a dime to each of the men so they could sleep in a bed for the night. Msgr. Jobs received this money by saying Mass on weekends at other churches; then, he promptly divided that income into dimes. The men came daily to receive their well-needed dime. Often, they were lined up all across the express-way...especially during the colder season. One of the men was called *Singing Sam*, because he used the overpass as a stage and entertained the others with his singing while they waited in line.

* * * * *

PUTNAM-MERRICK COOPERATIVE - When I became Pastor of Holy Trinity, I also inherited two homes that formed the Putnam-Merrick Cooperative. The men living there were able to pool their resources and live comfortably. They did well for many years, but the Co-op had eventually served its purpose. The last man to live there was Verne LaBranche. To him it was his home for life; he still lives there. In view of the situation, I awarded the home to Verne in 1993 for one dollar.

The Putnam bank account of $5,000.00 was also given to Verne. This money was used to pay taxes, utilities, and the general upkeep of the house. The Merrick house was then given to the Vietnamese men living there!

PART TWO

LA SED - SERVING THE HISPANIC COMMUNITY

16. FORMING THE HISPANIC TEAM

I expect to pass through this world but once. Any good thing, therefore, that I can do, or any kindness I can show a fellow being, let me do it now. Let me not defer or neglect it, for I shall not pass this way again.

-Stephen Grellet

LA SED is an acronym for "Latin Americans for Social and Economic Development." Today it is very current and active, but somehow it's exact history has been clouded in mystery. I believe it is time — actually long over due — to present the events that led to its existence. Although it is known to have started in 1969, the idea, you might say, began with a letter to Cardinal Dearden in 1967. At first, there seems to be no connection; however, the following clarifies the path that led from one event to the other.

Since I had been sent by the Archdiocese of Detroit to Mexico and to Puerto Rico to study Spanish and to become familiar with Hispanic Culture, each of my assignments included working with Spanish-speaking parishioners. While I was at Holy Cross Church in the Southwest area of Detroit called Delray, I sent in a plan to Cardinal Dearden concerning the non-directed and isolated work being done by each of the

185

priests working in parishes where Spanish was spoken. I offered a new approach with a goal of organizing all of the existing programs into one all-encompassing program for Southwest Detroit.

The Cardinal agreed and sent me to St. Bernadette in southeast Dearborn for six months to begin the effort of combining all Spanish-speaking programs into what would become *The Latin Ecclesial Team or The Latin Apostolate.*

At that time, in the sixties we used the word *Latin* for *Hispanic*, the future title for those in Spanish-speaking countries. I received the approval from Cardinal Dearden on June 20, 1967. I was delighted! I left Holy Cross Church and began living at St. Bernadette Church and working full time to establish united program to serve the Hispanic Community in Detroit and Ecorse. I began with three other priests in the Archdiocese: Fr. Larry Dunn, Fr. Jim Barret, a Redemptorist priest, and Fr. Broussard, a member of the Basilian Religious

186

Order. Included in the proposal to the Archbishop, was the request for a team of priests, Religious Sisters and lay persons to make contact with the Latins of Detroit who were either abandoning their affiliation with the Catholic Church, because of the language barrier or were actually being won over by Ministers of other faiths because of the personal interest shown to them.

We were able to join a group of Nuns who were Missionary Catechists from the same city where I first learned Spanish; namely, Tlapan, Mexico, a suburb of Mexico City. They were Sr. Enriqueta (the Superior), Sr. Maria Paz, Sr. Ramona and Sr. Rosario. However, almost from the beginning, the team was separated. The Sisters were previously committed to a program of working with migrants in rural areas, and the priests went to Mexico for the primary purpose of forming a team among themselves, as it was most difficult to do so in Detroit, where we all live in different Parishes and all were Associate Pastors.

While we were in Mexico preparing to function as a team, we also studied Spanish and Mexican Culture at the Center of Intercultural Formation in Cuernavaca, Mexico. The Sisters, in the meantime, had been making efforts to grow into a team as well. Unfortunately, Fr. Broussard, being a Basilian, was unable to go to Mexico that summer because of the General Chapter of the Basilian Order concurrently held.

Being back in Detroit, we resumed our meetings in September and realized that we had made great strides in working together. We met three times a week, studying Scripture and planning activities. By November, one lay couple had been added to the team: Alfredo and Lupe Aguirre. We were also at the point of adding three more couples. The reason for the four couples is the nature of our work and the extent of the area. In true post-conciliar fashion, we planned to make contact with any Hispanic individual or group of people by the combined work of the clergy, Religious and lay people.

It was obvious to us from the beginning that this well-intentioned, apostolic effort would be transcending parish boundaries and uniting natural, basic communities. This new arrangement offered one possible solution, but at the same time, presented a few unique problems. Among them was putting together a Staff large enough to reach the many thousands of Hispanic families scattered throughout Southwest Detroit.

Our goal never wavered from our original purpose — serving the Hispanic Community. It would be a gross misunderstanding to think that we were in any way encouraging Spanish-speaking people to strengthen themselves by banding together and thus isolate them even further from the rest of the community. Our ultimate goal, actually, was not to build a separate community, but rather to unite the Hispanic families first, then to completely integrate them with the other American people, regardless of race, color or creed.

We, therefore, had to re-structure the whole area, dividing it into four sectors. It was both coincidental and convenient that each of the priests on the team lived in one of the sectors. Since this was so, each of us would confine the majority of our efforts to the Hispanics in our particular area, working in collaboration with the surrounding Pastors.

17. BIBLE CIRCLES -

OUR SOURCE OF

INSPIRATION

Miracles are not

contrary to Nature,

but only contrary to what

we know about Nature.

-St. Augustine

In the sixties, there was so much stress on Biblical Theology that the team decided to arrange and adopt our own method of sharing the Gospel message. The Word of God, studied with openness to the Gospel results in an exciting experience and personal awareness of our relationship to the community and to an ever-deepening oneness in Christ. Jesus put it this way: "Where two or three of you are gathered together in my name, there I am in the midst of you." Matthew:18-20.

This, then, was precisely the origin of the *Bible Study Groups* or *Bible Circles,* which we set up in various locations to bring Christ to others. The rationale of Bible Circles may also be stated this way, as expressed in the Documents of the Vatican Council II on Revelation, Chap. 22-25: "Easy access to Sacred Scripture should be provided for all the Christian Faithful...to learn by frequent reading of the Divine Scriptures the 'excelling knowledge' of Christ. *For ignorance of the Scriptures is ignorance of Christ.*"

Each Bible Circle was conducted by a leader, previously trained in a Bible School, where a deeper study of the Scriptures takes place. The Word of God, being so dynamic and vibrant, because of the message it carries, forces people to act one way or the other. So far, we had only witnessed a positive reaction in all the Study Groups.

Our Ecclesial Team expanded, of course. We eventually became well-known throughout the Hispanic Community working closely with other priests, Fr. Kern included. We also became involved in a new movement which originally came to Detroit from Spain called a *Cursillo*. It was taught on the property of St. Leo Parish in Detroit and in Spanish. Its purpose was to awaken our responsibilities as Christians, through a meaningful and exciting expression of the Sacraments and the Liturgy. It also stirred up an emotional response deep within the soul. We also included a Married Couples Retreat called a *Marriage Encounter*. It was highly successful right from the beginning.

Our Team was growing fast! We reached hundreds of Latinos/Hispanos through the Annual Celebration of Our Lady of Guadalupe.

Every parish having a Guadalupe Society participated in this joyful celebration in honor of Jesus' Mother, who appeared to Juan Diego in 1531 and brought about the conversion of Mexico almost over night. Having such a joyful Mass Celebration — standing room only — including the Mariachis led by Salvador Torres and a full Mexican Dinner following, it was big and unforgettable for both Mexican and non-Mexican. The *salsa, composed mostly of jalapeños,* was not easy to forget either! This festive occasion was sponsored by the Comité Festejos Guadalupanos. They did a great job and also offered us numerous contacts each year.

Help also came from the Damas Catolicas, more or less equivalent to an Altar Society, which is still active in some parishes, as well as the Third Order of St. Francis in Spanish.

By 1969, we felt that we were over our heads in work. Our principal focus began as a purely spiritual work. Now we were overwhelmed with other needs not foreseen. Some of the people we served had financial problems, others needed a license or classes to learn English, getting on Welfare, counseling, a GED, a job, healthcare, food, etc. There was no end to the problems that we encountered in our home visits.

We became deadlocked at a certain point! How could we take care of their spiritual needs and fulfill their basic ones as well. We neither had the time nor the energy to do both.

By this time, we had twelve Bible Circles meeting regularly. Our Ecclesial Team was involved with the Guadalupe Societies and many other parish groups where the Spanish-speaking Community had to be served. In those days, Masses in Spanish were not widely celebrated yet. Since the Vatican Council encouraged Mass in the vernacular, it was a change of huge proportions for us. We immediately made plans to have a Mass in Spanish every Sunday in two or

195

three key areas. One was at St. Anne's (already in operation), at Holy Redeemer Church and at St. Francis Xavier Church in Ecorse. We slowly made plans to apply the privilege of having Mass in the home, but it would take place only when a certain group of people had been sufficiently instructed in the Word of God, the Sacraments, and the nature of the Mass as a true expression of Worship. In this way, our prayers and services would give real meaning to what our first Pope said in I Peter: 2-9, "You are a chosen race, a royal priesthood, a consecrated nation, a people set apart to sing praises of God."

Our Ecclesial or Latin Apostolate Team now consisted of seventeen members. Our days were filled with activities...often overloaded. What should we do? How do we handle the intake of increasing circumstances now beyond our time and energy? We had a goal in mind and we were very close. Our decision was to take a day off and have a complete Day of Recollection. The

Lord would surely guide us. For a Scripture reading we chose the Chapter 6: 1-6 of *The Acts of the Apostles* in the New Testament. It reads:

"In those days, as the number of disciples grew, the ones who spoke Greek complained that their widows were being neglected in the daily distribution of food, as compared with the widows of those who spoke Hebrew. The Twelve assembled the community of the disciples and said, 'It is not right for us to neglect the Word of God in order to wait on tables. Look around among our own number, brothers, for seven men acknowledged to be deeply spiritual and prudent, and we shall appoint them to this task. This will permit us to concentrate on prayer and the Ministry of the Word. The proposal was unanimously accepted by the Community. Following this they selected Stephen, a man filled with faith and the Holy Spirit; Philip, Prochorus, Nicanor, Timon, Parmenas, and Nicolaus of Antioch, who had been a convert to Judaism. They

presented these men to the Apostles, who
first prayed over them and then imposed
hands on them.' "

18. OUR FIRST MEETING

WAS A TOTAL FAILURE

BUT WE LEARNED AND...

LA SED WAS BORN

One cannot step twice

into the same river.

-Heraclitus

We were excited to find our answer in the Word of God. The Apostles had the same problem we had. They resolved their pressing issues by selecting help from among the Community. Seven good men! They blessed them and laid hands on them making them Deacons. The Deacons gave witness by handling the proper distribution of food and other family situations. By doing this, they freed up the Apostles to continue their spiritual work without interruption.

We felt it necessary to do the same thing...let the concerns of food, lodging, learning English, etc. be taken care of by a group of lay people. Our Ecclesial Team could be free to spread the Gospel and concentrate on spiritual matters. Before that was possible, we felt it necessary to invite all of the organizations speaking Spanish to a meeting. From that larger meeting we would surely find someone to take charge of the program to assist fellow Hispanics having a variety of needs. The least that we expected was that we could meet the leaders and work with them to a certain extent.

Naturally, we included the Guadalupe organizations already established in several parishes. There were other men and women Societies and Fraternities throughout the area, but some not directly connected with the Church. A few of them were: LAUPA or

Latin Americans United for Political Action, Latin Americans at Great Lakes Steel, Comité Patriótico Mexicano, Círculo Mutualista, Caballeros Católicos, Comité Restauradora Mexicana, Post 505 Mexican American Legion, L.A. Democratic Club, and Club Feminino.

By the end of the day, we mailed an invitation to all of the Spanish-speaking organizations to a general meeting. There were twenty-nine separate organizations in Southwest Detroit at the time. Each group was invited to send at least two officers as representatives of their organization to this meeting. The location we chose was a meeting room in the Holy Trinity School building. When the time for the meeting arrived, we grew very excited about this untried-before adventure. It was now past 7:00 p.m. Almost 7:15 p.m. Not one person showed up yet. Thinking that was maybe a custom among them that they come a little late to the meeting — like mañana — we continued to wait. After an hour, we realized that we did something wrong. We may have even offended the leaders of these Hispanic Programs. So we had to re-group. Back to square one! We concluded that just receiving a letter is too impersonal; each group should be contacted in person. We therefore divided up the list among us, each visiting the officers of a few of the organizations.

That was a lesson we all learned early in our Ministry. *Personal* contact meant *in person!*

Another date was planned. Again, surprisingly all twenty-nine organizations were represented! It was a great meeting. Never before had such a meeting taken place. I began by welcoming them and leading them in prayer. I shared a brief history how we came to that point and why they were invited. We needed help. It was time for the lay folks to take on the leading role in serving their brothers and sisters. First, we needed a name. What would we call this newly established group. I suggested using an *acronym*. I have always been fascinated with acronyms. In fact, I use them even to this day as an outline of my homilies. If I had four points to my talk, I would make up a word that encompassed the four ideas. Regardless of how many points I would make, I always came up with a word.

But to find a word for a group about to come into existence, we first needed to find a word that meant what we were about. Many words were suggested; very few appeared attractive. When our efforts tended to become tedious, I finally put the three most popular acronyms on the blackboard to vote on. *LA SED* was the unanimous choice. I am not sure who first suggested it, but it was a good one. It said precisely what we were attempting to accomplish: to help Latin Americans for Social and Economic Development. The Spiritual matters...our Ecclesial Team would handle. LA SED literally means *thirst*, but in a general sense, according to the Dictionary, it could mean a strong desire or craving...like a hunger and thirst for something. In this instance, LA SED would mean "Hispanics pursuing justice, equality, fairness and acceptance socially and economically."

At the conclusion of our decision, which described name and purpose of the newly-born LA SED, I then told this large group of active officers and representatives that I was withdrawing as Chairman of the meeting. It was time to vote for a Chairperson and a Co-chairperson. A lot of candidates were suggested; when it was over, it came to one person as their choice: Gus Gaynett. His Co-chair was Joe Lopez. I then resigned as Chairperson and handed over the official authority to Mr. Gaynett, who conducted the rest of the meeting. LA SED began its existence at that moment!

The next step was finding a place. Sherlock Holmes couldn't have done better. They found the perfect spot to house the LA SED operation...a former bank on W. Vernor in Southwest Detroit in the heart

Fr. Jay and Mary Turner, Field Representative

of the Mexican Community. It had recently closed. The only problem was getting the seed money to purchase the building. We would apply for financial assistance from the Archdiocese of Detroit. Joe Lopez, Gus Gaynett and I made an appointment with the Archdiocesan Development Fund a forerunner for the present CSA (Catholic Services Appeal). We were told by someone in advance that it was not going to be easy to get the money. That made us determined all the more! Joe Lopez spoke on our behalf, making a very strong appeal. Gus and I also added our verbal support. After fielding questions by the Board of Directors, we stepped out while they voted. It was very close but our request was granted. With $40,000 we purchased the building and began LA SED.

Today, LA SED continues after thirty-four years. It has gone far beyond our original

Senior Food Program at
LA SED

Kids at LA SED at Christmas Time

concept. It is now funded by the United Way Community Services, Detroit Area Agency on Aging, Police Athletic League, the City of Detroit, MDOT, Ford Motor, St. Vincent de Paul, Comerica and Myron P. Levin and other foundations, corporations and private donations. It still remains a non-profit agency serving Hispanics and residents of Southwest Detroit. It now assists people of all ages with a variety of bilingual services. They also address issues that affect the diverse ethnic groups living in that community.

These are some of their services:

FOR YOUTH: Tutoring, leadership training, educational counseling and financial aid information, school and Court advocacy, crisis intervention, summer Youth employment programs and GED preparation classes.

FOR SENIORS: Transportation to and from the Center and also for shopping, light housekeeping tasks, meal preparation, laundry and ironing services, minor home repairs, food and friendship Monday through Thursday, health screening services, arts and crafts, English classes, exercise, History of Detroit, sewing classes, social and emotional support, and finally, educational and recreational programs.

I am amazed how far they have come. LA SED was placed in the right hands: Dedicated people helping people! The various Staffs that have taken charge since the beginning of LA SED have continually risen to new and practical levels of people serving people. They are God's helpers pouring out their gifts and talents for the Hispanic Community of Detroit. I can only speak of their wonderful work with pride and gratitude.

PART THREE

LIGHTHOUSE: A BLESSING

OF LIGHT AND HOPE

19. MORE OF GOD'S

HUMBLE TEACHERS...

TO BE SERVED!

Oh, Keeper of the Lighthouse,
teacher and friend

Your beacon of help and love you
extend;

You model the strength and care of
your ways

In the darkest of night or

brightest of days.

-Kathleen Carolin

The least pain in

our little finger

gives us more concern than the

destruction of millions of lives.

-William Hazlitt

My priesthood seemed to center a round people in great need of help...both spiritual and material. Probably everyone needs assistance when it comes to general needs, but I am specifically talking about families and individuals who find themselves in substandard conditions.

When our Team for families of Hispanic origin moved out of the way and enjoyed having lay folks helping lay folks, it was a pleasure to watch LA SED operate so successfully without us. To me, that is the essence of true leadership: to move out of the way and allow people to take care of themselves. Demanding that those helped or guided rely on you always and everywhere certainly reflects more on self-interest than genuine service. As the old saying goes: *don't just give them a fish...teach them how to fish!*

In my first book, *On My Way Home*, I expressed how I reluctantly moved from St. Bernadette Church in Southeast Dearborn to St. Michael Church in Pontiac. Cardinal

Dearden, personally told me how the Arab people in the area wanted me to remain at St. Bernadette Church even though they were of the Muslim Faith. He was shocked — and so was I — when a bus load of Arabs came to the Archbishop's Office in Downtown Detroit to try to persuade him to allow me to stay in Southeast Dearborn. Regardless, the decision for me to be transferred was already made and it was not to be changed at that point. I had grown very fond of the Arab Community, but, reluctantly, it was time to move on. So, I moved up to the city of Pontiac, about twenty-five miles north of Detroit. Pontiac was also the heart of Pontiac Motors.

The Pastors following me at St. Bernadette would have to continue the cooperation and endearment of the Arab Community living in that same area. They certainly did the best they could in a fast changing neighborhood. As it turned out, the entire Parish Property is now in the hands of Arabic Organizations...and rightly so!

The Catholic families living in that portion of Southeast Dearborn had diminished in numbers year by year, until the parish church was no longer viable.

As far as my work in Pontiac was concerned, I saw it as a smaller version of Detroit and I was sent to care for the Hispanic Community once again. I have included much of my Pontiac assignment in my first book, but I did not mention an important program that developed in Pontiac as a service to the underprivileged. Back to "en servicio se encuentra la alegria" or "in service is found happiness." The Center in the Pontiac area was eventually called Lighthouse and I was happy to be a part of it, even in a small measure.

How, then, did a simple Parish service develop into such a huge organization? From its onset, no one could have predicted what an enormous future was in store for this rather ordinary program that cost very little to operate. Yet, today, *Lighthouse of Oakland County, Inc,* — according to

214

the latest audit — has an annual Operating Revenue of over $7 million and provides nearly 70,000 services by Staff and many volunteers. Moreover, there are Lighthouse Emergency Services for low/limited income seniors and families, near-homeless families, infants, children and youth in Oakland County. And that is only *one* subsidiary!

Lighthouse truly had humble beginnings. Sometimes, the greatest blessings begin with a tiny spark of light. Lighthouse began, unofficially, when individuals or families seeking help showed up at the back door of St. Vincent Convent in Pontiac, Michigan. Sr. Jean Ann Campana, a member of the Immaculate Heart of Mary Religious Community, gave food out of Church funds set aside for that purpose. She probably had no idea whatsoever that she was becoming the founder of a huge operation of public service. How did this come about? Eventually, after providing food to the hungry, offering clothes was a natural consequence of serving others with little or no income. Of course, as the need appeared, so did the volunteers! This backdoor agenda continued to expand, allowing others to experience the joy and happiness of giving, sharing and serving.

Five volunteer ladies originally took charge of the Clothes Program. Aid from St. Hugo Parish in Bloomfield helped greatly to finance its beginnings. Both the food and the clothes programs outgrew their surroundings. The Program, later called Lighthouse, then moved to St. Frederick School, also in Pontiac. Shortly after, in 1972, Lighthouse became incorporated.

20. THE ROLE OF THE CLERGY IN THE HUMBLE BEGINNINGS OF LIGHTHOUSE.

Who is wise?

One who learns from all.

-The Talmud

Two years later, the Pontiac Ecumenical Ministry came into the picture. The Pontiac Ecumenical Ministry at first consisted of three members: Reverends Jim Sheehan, Ed Rowe, and Eddie McDonald. It came into existence with the bussing situation in Pontiac. At the time, there was a federal case being decided in the Supreme Court of Michigan. The topic was *forced integration of schools by bussing.* There were strong opponents to this proposal on both sides. Apparently those against integration resorted to violence. At one point, there was a bomb on a school bus stationed in the parking lot.

When school started under the guidance of Rev. Ed Rowe, many Ministers got on board and traveled the busses with the children to protect them and to ward off violence. The clergy of Pontiac became united and organized out of that *defense-of-the-children* project. Their purpose expanded quickly: *to get people to unite with other people* — especially their own parishioners and to set the standard for the rest of the community.

I was happy to be an active member of the Pontiac Ecumenical Ministry (also known as the PEM). Included were clergy of varying Faiths: Reverends Ed Rowe, United Methodist, John Hooper, Catholic; (both taking leading roles on behalf of the clergy) David Brower, Episcopal; Eddie McDonald, Friendship Missionary Baptist; James Sheehan, Catholic; Richard Chilcott, Lutheran; Doris Brown, Friendship Missionary Baptist, Roger Derby, Episcopal; Earl Beck, Missouri Synod Lutheran; Leonard Munson and a Rabbi, whose name I do not recall. There were others!

We served our parishioners and poor families with the same goals we all seek. One of them is the deep spiritual joy that is a natural result of service. We, as Clergy, were delighted when we gathered for a meeting, representing the whole city of Pontiac. We never argued religion. That would be a meaningless task. We were all confident in our religious vocation, believing that each of us were called by God. Rather, we spoke of activity, projects, plans, strategy and inter-faith religious ceremonies that would benefit our own congregations as well as the poor, the underprivileged and the unchurched. It comes down to the same theme: One's soul is filled with an exceptional cheerfulness in sharing our Faith through religious love put into action.

After a successful effort on the part of the Pontiac Clergy, the Pontiac Ecumenical Ministry was formed and began to have regular meetings and was especially concerned about the increasing number of low-income and no-income families and individuals in the city of Pontiac.

Lighthouse, at that time, was a fledgling organization but very real and a very effective source of assistance for the poorer class. Since the origin of Lighthouse was connected to a church setting, the PEM was destined to become the umbrella organization supporting and promoting Lighthouse. On the other hand, Lighthouse Staff always wanted to be independent, but at this time the opportunity was present for their organization to utilize the incomparable talents and abilities of the Clergy: they were natural leaders, organizers, counselors and dedicated spiritual servants, maintaining the highest respect of their own congregations and, in general, the city of Pontiac.

In this initial stage, Myra Kreuger was Director of Lighthouse. Under her leadership, Lighthouse moved forward quickly in its new partnership with the Pontiac Ecumenical Ministry. Its purpose, its direction and expansion grew beyond anyone's dreams. Thanksgiving and Christmas Programs were soon included besides daily assistance. Shortly after, Helen Fitzgerald became Director as Myra Kreuger had gone on to found the Women's Survival Center.

In the beginning, Lighthouse reported to the Pontiac Ecumenical Ministry and the Board of Directors, which consisted mainly of volunteers from the different churches. Besides becoming deeply involved in the work of Lighthouse, the Pontiac Ecumenical Ministry had earned the reputation of successfully fulfilling its role as *Advocate for Social Justice in Pontiac.*

Food pantry at Lighthouse

The need for independence was becoming an issue and so the first stages of separating Lighthouse from PEM began around 1980 and a complete separation took place in 1981. The efforts and accomplishments of Lighthouse and the Pontiac Ecumenical Ministry were both very noble and they were a great team together; however, their goals began to move in opposite directions.

Both were serving the general Community, but in a different manner. The Pontiac Ecumenical Ministry began to unite itself closely with the Pontiac Citizens' Coalition (PCC), which was strongly opposed to redlining (in which a bank becomes exacting and selective against loans to the poorer classes) and the Hospital issue, in which the PCC fought against Pontiac General Hospital moving out of the city. There were also Black and Hispanic racial issues and other civic affairs...sometimes involving picket lines.

In a word, the PEM was becoming more and more political in its directives. In contrast, Lighthouse maintained its goals of Emergency Services providing quality service of food and clothing to the poor, Housing Projects and a variety of Programs, representing a totally different approach according to its mission statement. Rev. David Brower became Director during this time to assure the stability of Lighthouse and its Services.

21. LIGHTHOUSE,

ON ITS OWN,

MOVED INTO THE FUTURE

OF TOTAL SERVICE.

We need people

who can dream

of things that never were

and ask why not.

-George Bernard Shaw

After a couple of years, while making progress daily in its efforts to be of service, Lighthouse began searching for a new Director. There were several candidates. Noreen Keating, who started as a volunteer and was promoted to a part-time Assistant Director in 1982, was chosen from among other candidates and has been the Chief Executive Officer up to the time of this writing, 2004. She has been and still is a great blessing to the operation of Lighthouse, the largest provider for Emergency Services in Oakland County.

Most senior citizens were connected to Lighthouse and got more volunteers. Emergency food was given highest priority, especially for the Annual Holidays. At Thanksgiving time, over 7,000 people were fed, a far cry from the twenty-five families who were given food baskets at the onset of the Lighthouse Operation years before. Volunteer rehabilitation was also part of Lighthouse's success, offering instruction in managing the family budget and financial affairs.

In 1982, Lighthouse moved to the Dutch Colonial Home next to All Saints Episcopal

Church. It then moved to the corner of Williams Street and Orchard Lake Rd. Headed by Jack Fitzgerald, all the buildings, including the interior and the electrical work, were finished by volunteers.

At first, just churches helped. For example, at St. John Fisher chapel, the Pastor stood in the back collecting checks after their talk about Lighthouse. In 1983, the Board of Directors became aware of an article in the local newspaper concerning grants to be offered by the Robert Wood Johnson Foundation. Helen Fitzgerald, a Board member at that time, encouraged the Board to compose a grant. In March of 1984, with a very limited number of grants being offered, Lighthouse qualified for a grant. Receiving that grant was important to Lighthouse, giving it a name and status in its financial operation of service. Support continued and expanded.

Later, Skillman and United Way gave even greater credibility and substance to Lighthouse. Among the Annual Grants, the largest came from Skillman: approximately one million dollars! United Way was a big help as well. Another dream became fulfilled...an active Montessori Child Care Program was started and is still in operation.

Generous donations then came from a variety of sources: New Home Revenue, Governmental Agencies, Individuals and Corporations, Special Events, Foundations, Churches — and donated goods and services continued poured in. With the financial situation in place, volunteers were still needed for personal contact and continue to be the backbone of the operation of Lighthouse. As with Holy Trinity Church, where I was once assigned, Lighthouse continues to this day to receive as they give. There seems to be a *Universal Law of Giving and Receiving.*

In 1990, Lighthouse set up another Emergency Services Center in Clarkston, as well as in Pontiac, to meet the growing needs in the larger community. Some of

227

Lighthouse (2004)

the needs in Clarkston varied in nature from those in Pontiac. Besides the huge Christmas Program in Clarkston, there were emergencies concerning medical prescriptions, mortgage payments, and being over-extended on house payments and utilities.

Members on the Lighthouse Staff, knowing that I followed Fr. Kern as Pastor of Holy Trinity Church, reminded me that Fr. Kern once drove up to Pontiac to give a talk on Justice and Peace. *He was one of God's servants speaking to other servants of*

228

God. It was a cold, rainy day and the group waited quite a while for him; he finally arrived quite late. He gave his talk and never mentioned that he had a flat tire on the Lodge Freeway. That had to be a very difficult situation for him, changing a tire on the Lodge is nothing short of dangerous, not to mention the possibility of being hit by a car or even mugged. Typical of Fr. Kern, he never said a word about it...until someone mentioned something about his delay in getting there.

The Lighthouse Staff has many reasons to be proud of their accomplishments. Here is just one of their reasons: *Lighthouse of Oakland County was the winner of the 1997 Crain's Best-Managed Nonprofit Contest* for non-profits with a budget of more than $3 million. Eighty-nine percent of Lighthouse Revenue goes directly toward services for those in need. In March of that same year, Lighthouse asked actor Tim Allen, whose mother and step-father were volunteers for Lighthouse, to accept being chairperson

229

for a planned capital campaign. He did accept and *Tim Allen raised more than $100,000* for them when his movie *Jungle 2 Jungle* actually premiered in Detroit.

When I was a member of the Pontiac Ecumenical Ministry back in the 1970's, I knew K. Noreen Keating, one of its volunteers. Noreen had great potential! She was first asked to drop off food; since then, she has followed a very successful journey of service. She became a part-time Assistant Director in 1982; the budget was only $200,000 at that time. She is now the CEO or President of Lighthouse whose total assets, including an Endowment are valued nearly $12 million. She heads three separate business units each with a separate Board of Directors: *Lighthouse Emergency Services*, *Lighthouse Path* and *Lighthouse Community Development.*

It would literally take an entire book to write a detailed, historical description of this remarkable organization, appropriately called Lighthouse. What I have written is simply a sketchy review of a few highlights in its jam-packed history.

Two years ago, the present Lighthouse building was ready and began its operation where it now stands. It is a magnificent building with a huge Lighthouse standing in front of it. The actual lighthouse is truly a beacon to those who are looking for help. I was fortunate to have even a small role in such a big operation of service.

May the beacon of light and hope continue for many years to serve those who come to its doors for help...and are welcomed to walk in.

PART FOUR

MY BLOODLINE

GOING BACK

TO THE EARLY

17TH CENTURY

22. THE MAN WHO WOULD

BE POPE!

...MY UNCLE.

Love treats all alike,

knowing no seasons, nor climate,

nor hours, nor days or months

which are the rags of time.

-John Donne

The above is a true statement. It sounds rather bold and arrogant. I feel the same response as I did when I first heard about "The Man Who would be King." But that is precisely what happened. I was born into a Lebanese Maronite Catholic family with a long history of vocations to the priesthood and to the Religious Sisterhood. The family history goes further back than I can address, but there is ample information about some of my uncles who became famous during their lifetime. I realize fully that this is no particular credit to me since I was simply born into that heritage, but I do find it fascinating that one of my uncles left his mark in the world. He was an Archbishop and a true servant of God.

I included a few thoughts about my family tree in my first book, *On My Way Home*. On the occasion of my ordination to the priesthood in 1956 in Detroit, Michigan by his Eminence, Cardinal Edward Mooney, thoughts of my family tree raced through my mind. My father often spoke of his uncles who were Bishops, authors and had been in charge of the Vatican Library. It never occurred to me that I came from a family tree adorned with uncles who held high posts in a Church over 2,000 years old. But on the very day and during the Ceremony of my ordination, I reflected strongly on how I joined my ancestors in the priesthood of Jesus Christ!

Since this book is designed to record how *service is happiness*, I believe one of my uncles was a servant who found happiness in his work; the work of serving God, the Church and the people who would benefit from his presence and his voluminous writings. Though Archbishop Assemani's light and fame shined high above his relatives, this Assemani family originating in the small village of Hasroun in Lebanon produced an extraordinary number of Bishops, Diocesan Priests, Franciscan Monks and Nuns.

I have three sources from which to draw the knowledge and information that follows. The first was the custom in our family to talk about our *roots* and to discuss information about our ancestors; most of this knowledge came through tradition by word of mouth. My uncles, being related to each other, passed down a considerable amount of information about the Assemani family and the special events in their lives. My dad made several trips to Lebanon and was very familiar with the history of our family tree. The second source was what I read in the Catholic Encyclopedia about four of my uncles who were all Bishops and their relationship to each other as brothers or uncle and nephew.

The following are some of my uncles:
The brother of Joseph Simon Assemani was
Bishop Josephus Aloysius Assemani, who
was born in Tripoli, Lebanon in 1710 and
died in 1782 in Rome, Italy. He also had
a post in the Vatican Library and was an
extensive writer, authoring many books.
Their nephew was Archbishop Stephanus Evodius
(or Awwad) who was born in 1707 and died
in 1782. He wrote many books as well and,
of course, also worked in the Vatican Library.
In addition, he also had the prestige of
being a member of the Royal Society of
London. A grand nephew of Joseph Simon
Assemani was Bishop Simeon, who was appointed
Professor of Oriental Languages at the
Seminary of Padua, Italy in 1785 and later,
in 1807, was appointed Professor at the
University of Padua. He, too, has authored
books well known in the Mideast.

The last of these five bishops I met,
not in person, but through letter-writing.
He was fluent in eleven languages. I could
have easily written to him in English,

but I chose to write in the modern language I was studying at Sacred Heart Seminary in Detroit. It was French, which I found to be a beautiful language. I had my Seminary Professor check it before I put it in the mail. He said there was nothing to correct.

Shortly after, I received a letter written in French from Lebanon. My uncle, Archbishop Louis Assemani, actually wrote back to me. I couldn't believe the magnificent script of a ninety year old man. His writing was clear and consisted of beautiful flowing lines like I had never seen. Also included in the letter was a long message for my dad in Arabic. Whether the Arabic writing was outstanding or not, I had no idea. To me it looked like shorthand; however, my dad translated it for me and they were beautiful words.

I believe that was a year or so just before my uncle died in 1950. I was ordained six years later. Was I following a long line of Bishops? It never occurred to me! Nor have I ever desired to be a Bishop.

I was happy just being a simple priest working in the inner city of Detroit. The line of Bishops ended with my last Bishop/uncle, Archbishop Louis Assemani of Lebanon. His brother, also my uncle, was the Superior General of the Black Friars (Franciscans) of Lebanon.

I happened to be a direct, blood-line nephew of these noble and illustrious Clergymen.

The third source of information was a biographical sketch delivered by the Abbot John Moharbis in 1968. It was the 200th anniversary of Archbishop Joseph Simon Assemani's death. This occasion was celebrated in festive pageantry. I was given a copy of Abbot Moharbis' twenty-eight page booklet by Fr. Dahdah, a priest from Lebanon, who took up residence and parish work in the Archdiocese of Detroit. He said, "This is the biography of one of your uncles and you should have it." I was very grateful to him for such a meaningful gift; however, when I opened the booklet, it was all in

Arabic. I laughed! I said, "What can I do with this? I don't read Arabic." He replied that he would translate it for me. He did, even though it had to be tedious. (I was shocked when I first went to an Arabic Organization in Dearborn to have it translated and they said it would cost me $1,000. Fr. Dahdah did it out of the goodness of his heart!)

The chronicle of my uncle who would be Pope focuses on Joseph Simon Assemani (in Arabic: Al Semaani). He became the companion of Popes and advocate to the heirs of Prince Fakher-El-Dine Elmahny the Great.

He was not only prolific in his writings — well over one hundred volumes in many different languages — but he wrote on so many different topics. He was well-versed not only on religious subjects, but also in the field of science and academic and scholastic studies.

Joseph Simon Assemani, was a Maronite Bishop. (I, too, was born a Maronite or Eastern Catholic. Before ordination, I changed to the Latin Rite of the Church.) Quoting Abbot Moharbis, this prestigious man "emerged from the land of Lebanon as a genius whose equal cannot be found in the world of Science for more than 200 years, was very useful to humanity in his talents, in his enduring energies and his writings. He was a pride to Maronite Catholics, to the city of Hasroun and to the noble Assemani family. Indeed, he is an object of pride for the Middle East. He is a great man of letters and a mighty man of science. A man of his culture is without equal. The results of his brilliant mind were overwhelming. His numerous and illustrious writings astonish the human mind!"

His legacy has endured to this day and into the future as strongly as it did in 1768. He stands as a blazing beacon for the future generations of students

Archbishop Joseph Simon Assemani

and as an incomparable source of knowledge
for the Orientalists (Middle East Scholars.)
He will always be considered a powerful
citizen, a man of letters, a great historian

and a Bishop without equal, who lived 81 years.

Abbot Moharbis goes on to say that the wide range of possible topics about this notable man is endless, based on the convincing facts, but that he will outline his article in three phases; (1) Introduction, his youth and its value (2) his scientific works (3) his final days and his services.

23. MY UNCLE'S EARLY

LIFE OF

LEARNING AND SERVICE.

All great things are simple,

and many can be expressed

in a single word:

freedom; justice; honor;

duty; mercy; hope.

-Winston Churchill

Joseph was born at the beginning of summer, 1687 in Tripoli, Lebanon, where his parents resided in winter. This bright, intelligent child learned Arabic, Syriac and started learning Latin at the age of eight. In 1695, the child Joseph Assemani was sent to Roman schools, to his cousin, Joseph Louis Semaani, to continue his education. He was always first among thousands of students in the final examinations.

Later, when word of Joseph Assemani's genius, intelligence and piety reached the ears of Pope Clement XI, he detained him, during the summer vacations, from leaving Rome for his native country Lebanon. The Pope proposed to Joseph that he re-catagorize the Middle East documents in the Vatican library! These documents had been offered by his relative, Bishop Elias Assemani, Pastor of a church in Antioch. The young Joseph Assemani immersed himself totally in what the Holy Father entrusted to him and did it with perfection, adding to each document a résumé of its contents. And he had written in collaboration with the Patriarch Simon Awad, while both were students, a book about the four Patriarchs of the Middle East. Yet he was only nineteen years old. These capabilities made him worthy of the title of Official Translator of the Oriental/Middle East Languages in the Vatican Library. This was March 10, 1710. July 1, of the same year, he earned a Doctorate in Philosophy and Theology, with a *Maxima cum Laude* in Moral and Dogmatic Theology.

When the Holy Father created a committee of scholars to refine the liturgies for the Oriental Churches, Assemani was on one of its working committees. Then, he started explaining articles and writings by extracting hidden treasures from the essence of these documents. With this, he created a new way for the Western world to become aware of Mideast Culture and its impressive Sciences. He put in writing the Natural Sciences, analyzing and synthesizing between Natural Philosophy and Theology in the interest of Christian Doctrine.

He called his work *The Book of Natural Sciences,* by Joseph, the Maronite, son of Shamoun, from the city of Hasroun. It was dedicated to the Monastery of St. Peter and St. Shaline in the year 1712, during the Papacy of Clement XI; thus, his scholarly abilities began to shine among scholars of scientific thought and literature. Assemani mastered the understanding, writing and speaking in twenty-five languages! Some said he knew thirty languages. When he reached this high level in knowledge, the Holy Father sent him to the Middle East in 1715 to collect the old Oriental (Mideast) books. He traveled through Egypt, Syria, Cypress and Lebanon despite the difficulties of travel at that time.

His compatriot, the Patriarch Jacob Awad, also from Hasroun, helped him to obtain several of them. He returned to Rome with about four hundred books of precious documents, containing one hundred and forty-three Syriac, Armenian and Chaldean manuscripts, ninety-five Coptic and Persian manuscripts and one-hundred and ninety-two Arabic and Greek ones which did serve him in his valuable and famous writings in the Oriental Library. On January 3, 1729, Pope Clement XII made him the first custodian of the Vatican Library, succeeding Bishop Carlos. Assemani was the first Lebanese named to this office. He gave it his best. He was then counted among the permanent officials of high-salaried positions at the Vatican State.

Then he started to rise in the Ecclesiastical Orders. He received Minor Orders in 1717. He was ordained a priest in 1719, and shortly after, his Degree in Canon Law. Not surprisingly, he was subsequently appointed the Pope's personal Secretary and Advisor.

24. ARCHBISHOP JOSEPH SIMON ASSEMANI: ADVISOR OF POPES, THE ROMAN CURIA, KINGS AND DIGNITARIES IN THE FIELD OF SCIENCE.

There are different kinds of spiritual gifts...

To one is given through the Spirit the expression of wisdom;

To another, the expression of knowledge..."

-1 Corinthians 12: 4-6

Just as a flower gives out its fragrance

to whomsoever approaches or uses it,

so love from within us radiates

towards everybody and manifests

as spontaneous service.

-Swami Ramdas

Assemani put aside the desire to achieve a high rank in order to give himself ever more passionately to Sciences and to personal holiness. His unique desire was to soar as high as an eagle. It was a continuing increase in his desire to fulfill his responsibility in a more perfect way, writing and publishing his manuscripts successfully to the point where even his friends did not know what to say when they talked about his accomplishments. This should not be surprising since his life was filled to overflowing in Sciences. His name gained widespread attention and reached the trust of his contemporaries, who were among the greatest scholars of the world at that time. His office became a gathering place for the educated class of writers and leading thinkers, especially scholars from the Middle East.

Many times, the Congregation of the Faith for the Mideast Churches would ask his advice and adopt his opinions, as did the Roman Rota and other Congregations. Pope Clement XII admired his abilities and named him his personal Secretary and Advisor. That was in 1733. Then, he named him one of the Bishops of his Diocese with the right to pontificate in 1735.

He sent him as his Vicar to the Maronite Church in Lebanon to preside over the Lebanese Council in 1736 with the purpose of re-organizing the Maronite Rite in collaboration with the Patriarch, the Bishops and the leaders of the community. This Council has remained a genuine one through the centuries. This same Pope entrusted to him a special Office reserved only for experts in Law and Justice in 1739.

Popes, Kings and the great ones of that time relied on Joseph Assemani and trusted him fully. We cannot describe enough how close Assemani was to Pope Benedict XIV. His Holiness treated him as a dear son. He would ask his advice concerning difficult subjects. Because of his loyalty, wisdom and vast knowledge, the Pope appointed him as the Personal Adviser to the Congregation of the Holy Office to help him in his continual and important writings. In 1755, the Pope appointed him as Director of the Archives for the Congregation of Penance. Later, he gave him the Office of the Seals in 1761 and in 1766, Assemani was consecrated as the Archbishop of Tyre in Lebanon.

Assemani did not only gain the favor of Popes, Religious leaders and the men of Science, but he also attracted the attention of Kings and other famous people of that time. History mentions that Charles IV, King of Naples and Sicily asked Assemani to write the history of his country, overlooking all the scholars in the West. The perfection of his work brought him close to the King, who bestowed on him the title of Honorary Citizen. These are but a few pictures of the important roles that only Assemani, and no other, was qualified to play.

Another comment from Abbot Moharbis: "It is extraordinary that Assemani in all the steps of his noble life, never gave in to the spirit of superiority, pride and arrogance.

"He was meek, calm and mild-mannered in his shining smile, no matter the multitude of his tasks. Would he be otherwise? He, who was the authoritative voice for all the Easterners: the Maronites, the Coptics, the Armenians, the Syrians, the Chaldeans, the Melkites and even for many leaders of Orthodox belief."

He really was the first and the last resort, the one to help them make a decision in their litigations.

It is a current saying that each language learned doubles the worth of the man. If Assemani understood, wrote and spoke twenty-five languages or thirty as some have said, what an incredible person he must have been! Was he not a human prodigy very seldom repeated?

His printed publications numbered one hundred-ten thick volumes, most of them concerning History. The first fruit of his labor was the Catalog for the Vatican Library and the Book of the Oriental Patriarchs.

Fortunately, his works that were published, are:

1. All Syriac, Arabic, Armenian documents and others in the Vatican Library. These comprehensive works are very important. They explore the Christian Arabic and Syriac Literature as well as many other Middle East manuscripts. These are among the best published works of Assemani in the opinion of the experts. To this day, in their entirety, they are still a primary source for Oriental researchers.

2. The translation of "The History of the Orient" by Peter the Monk from Arabic to Latin and added to it four lengthy articles, defining the Catholic thinking toward heretics. It was published in Venice in 1731.

3. The famous Lebanese Council and the Constitutional Law for the Maronite Church. He wrote it in Arabic and Latin and published it in 1736. This council magnificently organized the affairs of the Maronite Church at that time and all the Oriental Churches took their Laws from it. Assemani, as a representative of Pope

Clement XII, signed the Council Documents with the Patriarch, the Bishops, the Father Generals of Religious Orders and thirty-seven lay leaders.

4. The History of the Saints translated by Assemani from Greek to Latin in three volumes. It was published in 1727.

5. The written works of St. Ephraim the Syrian in three large Greek volumes were translated into Latin by Assemani, adding valuable prefaces and explanations. He also catalogued all the Greek and Syriac works of St. Ephraim which were published in Rome in 1732, 1733, and 1747.

6. An interesting article about the French Saint of Toscana.

7. A grammar in the Greek language and its subdivisions for students of all grades in two volumes; published in 1737.

8. Three official speeches he gave in St. Peter's Basilica at the burial services of Pope Benedict XIII and the

elevation to the Papacy of his successor. Also a Pastoral Encyclical on behalf of Pope Clement XII in which he explained the church rules and its official ceremonies, published in 1739, and a report he had taken of the regulations of a Papal council held on July 13, 1744.

At that time, Pope Benedict XIV confirmed the Patriarch Simon Awad on the Maronite Church, with letters to the Patriarch and Bishops. Assemani wrote the Ordinances and declarations of a Pontifical Council in 1742, the year Benedict confirmed Peter Wartabeet a Patriarch of Little Armenia and Cilicia and gave him the Pallium.

9. A translation of the monastic Rules and Constitution of the Maronite monks from Arabic into Latin, adding to them as an introduction to a magnificent Arabic letter published in 1735 and another letter to the Antonine monks (of St. Isaie) and another to the Basilian Melkite, including the Religious Sisters, published in 1741 and in 1764.

10. A Calendar of the universal Catholic Church in six large volumes published in 1751 and in 1753.

11. A History of Naples and Sicily, at the request of their King, Charles IV, in four volumes.

12. The Oriental Canon Law and Civil Law in four volumes, published in 1762, 1764 and in 1765.

13. An Arabic letter to the Basilian and Melkite Father General and his monks on the origin of their Religious Order and how it continued to spread, published in 1758.

In August of 1768, a huge fire occurred and destroyed the remaining manuscripts of Archbishop Joseph Assemani. Most of them were ready for publication:

1. The fifth volume of the Oriental library containing the Holy Scripture with Syriac and Arabic translations.

2. Seven authors of the church.

3. The seventh volume of the Syrian Councils.

4. The eighth volume of the Arabic Councils.

5. The ninth volume of the Greek writers whose books were translated into Syriac and Arabic.

6. The tenth volume on the Christian-Arab writers.

7. Volumes eleven and twelve on the Moslem writers.

8. An old Orthodox Calender.

9. The eighth volume on the Syrian /Lebanese-Maronites, the Jacobites and the Nestorians old Calender.

10. Three volumes on the old Calender of the Armenians, Egyptians, the Latins and Ethiopians.

11. The fifth and the sixth volumes of Naples and Sicily and other volumes on Italian history. Add to these are:

(a) Writings on the holy Icons and relics,

(b) Other writings on the holy Icons conserved on the old Latin and Greek manuscripts,

(c) another work he completed on the picture of Jesus Christ and His Mother,

(d) Another publication on the liturgies of the Maronite and Jacobite Church, including all the Heretics and the Oriental Councils in six volumes.

12. A manuscript on old and modern Syria in nine volumes, with a map of Syria, Palestine, Phoenicia and the other near-Eastern countries.

13. The Middle East History in nine volumes on the Maronites, the Melkites, the Druze, the Alawites, the Moslems, the Coptics, the Jacobites, the Ethiopians, the Nestorians and the Armenians.

14. A Syriac grammar, explaining Arabic and the explanation of the difficult verses in the Old and the New Testament.

Ever since I was a child, I had heard this story of the fire that destroyed the home of my uncle. My father, my uncle, the last of the Assemani Bishops, who died in 1950, two of my cousins who were Monsignors, and other priest-relatives and friends who were familiar with the Assemani Family, all said the same thing: there was a strong group of opponents to having a Lebanese Pope on the Throne of St. Peter. They deliberately set fire to his home demonstrating their opposition. Although Archbishop Assemani was ready to receive the red hat of a Cardinal and very likely to be elected the next Pope, he was urged by the Pope Benedict XIV to return to Lebanon for his own safety.

Assemani had been called by the Pope himself and high-ranking Cardinals as *Papabile* (meaning *likely to be Pope!*) In those days — as well as today — there were those who would *kill* to have their own religious beliefs or traditions preserved. Many today believe that Pope John Paul I was assassinated. It is a fact that Pope John Paul II was shot and nearly killed! I am not exaggerating when I say that my uncle would very likely have been chosen to be the next Pope at that time if his life were not threatened! If Popes were chosen by popular demand, he would have been the number one choice!

25. THE CITY OF HASROUN

IN LEBANON -

THE BIRTHPLACE OF MY

PARENTS, AND WELLSPRING

OF MANY GREAT

RELIGIOUS LEADERS.

Be thou faithful unto death,

and I will give you the

crown of life.

-Revelations 2:10

Here is what Abbot John Moharbis concluded in his talk on the 200th Anniversary of Assemani's passing. It is paraphrased since it was given in Arabic originally.

The reverence given to Archbishop Assemani by all the public and private officials is an historical fact. He was among the great ones...like a great conqueror. All the people and all the leaders of countries would talk about him with respect and admiration and would shower him with pleasant praises. We have seen how Charles IV, King of Sicily and Naples, was oblivious and unmindful of his own Western scholars and asked Joseph Simon Assemani to write for his country a Universal History and reserved for him the rank of Honorary Citizenship in 1739.

Pope Clement XII wrote to him in 1735, with these words, "To the beloved son Youssef Shamoun Al-Semaani (Joseph Simon Assemani), one of the principal authorities of our palace and our continued confidant and companion..." Also, in his letter to the

263

Maronite Patriarch, Youssef Al-Dhazen, the Pope said, "We are sending you with affectionate feeling — to answer your demand — a delegate from us, the beloved son, Joseph Assemani, who enjoys in our city the most powerful name in years because of his proven piety and intelligence, his knowledge and wisdom in Mideast affairs and especially in your territory."

Also, the Pope wrote to the Bishop of the Diocese with the same praise and reverence concerning Assemani. Pope Benedict XIV wrote to Assemani saying, "Beloved Son, peace and Apostolic blessing. What we think of you in the realm of high character and piety and progress in the Holy Sciences and Arts is not new, but it dates for thirty years. We have known you before we were elevated to the apostolic See (the Papacy) and remember the many generous Services to us and how much pain it has caused you. These praiseworthy qualities made us put you at the highest rank in our love and respect. The many and useful writings you published for the Middle East library did earn you, among all the nations, a great name, praise and fame that could never be erased in the many years and centuries to come."

Bishop Stefan Awad, his colleague in the Lebanese council, said of Joseph Simon Assemani, within the hearing of all, "He is the star of the Middle East. The Roman Church is entitled to be proud of him because the glory of Lebanon has been given to him. And our Maronite Church is entitled to beatify him as the Virgin Mary said "from this day forward all generations shall call me blessed."

Assemani held in his hand the civilization of fourteen centuries. Two-hundred years have passed since his death and his works are still the goal and guide of scholars. Very often, Pope Benedict XIV would read them. Pope Leo XIII had a passionate craving for his works, and in his Encyclical for the renewal of the Maronite College in Rome, wished for it to renew the creative times of the scholar, Assemani. Decy and other French scholars would bow their heads respectfully upon hearing his name.

The German Middle East Scholars declare even now that their unique teacher is Assemani and his Middle East Library. One of them, Theodore Noldik, wrote that Joseph Simon Assemani was considered as unequaled in his century. Msgr. Alfred Bodriard, in his speech at the Capital of Argentina, called the writings of Assemani "an incomparable great work." Cardinal Lipsier compares Assemani to a great ocean pouring incessantly with knowledge.

Bishop Youssef El-Dips in his story of Syria said of him: the writings of Assemani were so numerous that one diligent reader could not read them all. He is a Lebanese scholar with the goal to serve the world of Science and his country. Really, his works are a shining page in World History.

Abbot Moharbis continues: "Assemani lived eighty-one years in a continual, creative endeavor. He included in his Will the desire to be buried at the Maronite College in Rome. The burning of his library hastened, in three months, the drooping and weakening of his muscles and vitality. By the end of December, 1768, he gave up his pure soul."

This genius and Archbishop, Joseph Assemani, served through his learning and his pen both the East and the West. He served the Middle East by unfolding its ancient Civilization to the West. Archbishop Assemani served the whole world during his life and beyond. We are only seeing a tiny picture of a literary giant, since we have covered only a glimpse of his many works and accomplishments. Our deepest feelings should be admiration and pride towards this great man.

"People of the world, judge for yourselves! It is absolutely out of the question that fate would create another of his caliber and stature."

Hasroun, Lebanon is just one of many villages. However, it is easily distinguished by the fact that it has produced so many dedicated Bishops and Scholars. Most of the following were educated in the Maronite College of Rome and almost every one of them were related:

1. Bishop John Sandouk, born at the end of 1600, was appointed translator and interpreter for the Mideast languages at the royal palace of France.

2. Bishop John Hawshab, 1700.

3. Bishop Michael Sahade, 1669.

4. The Cor-Bishop Elias Semaani had collected, at the order of Pope Clement XI, Middle East documents for the Vatican library in 1700. He was a relative to Archbishop Joseph Assemani.

5. Patriarch Jacob Awad, a relative to Joseph Assemani, as well as to all the Awad Bishops.

6. Bishop Youseff Shamhoun Assemani, uncle to the great Assemani.

7. Patriarch Semaan Awad.

8. Bishop Stephan Awad, nephew of the great Assemani and his helper in the Vatican library.

9. Bishop Stephan Awad II, 1834.

10. Bishop Boulous Awad.

Before we complete this résumé of Archbishop Joseph Simon Assemani, we cannot help but draw a comparison between the number of clergy of Hasroun today and their number up to the beginning of the twentieth century. There is a depressing feeling in the throat! Times have changed radically, but the memory of Hasroun, cradle to its abundance of religious leaders, will never be forgotten. Its Patriarchs, Archbishops and Bishops exceeded, in those days, the number of twenty-five, besides its many Religious and Nuns.

"Finally, just as God has gratified the city of Hasroun with many great and beautiful individuals and scholars, in the religious and civil field, so the people poured on it distinguishing qualities and characteristics. Some have called Hasroun the *bride of the northern summer resort*; others, *the city of scholars*; still others, *the nest of eagles*. But, as with all great moments in History, that period of great scholars has ended.

The general contents of the above comments are supported by the older version of the Catholic Encyclopedia, which covers two pages describing the Assemani Bishops, particularly the works of Joseph Simon Assemani.

Also, in our circle of family, relatives and friends — all connected to the Assemani Family Tree — some of the above stories have been passed on to us many times. Added to that information, we were also told, ever since we were children, that Archbishop Assemani was not only in charge of the

Vatican Library, but was also officially named *Papal Secretary* at one point.

Regrettably, I only began to appreciate the enormous impact and influence of these noble Bishops and Scholars — all relatives by blood — in the latter part of my life. What I admire most is their dedication and total commitment to serve the Church and the world at large. Thank you, servants of the Lord.

EPILOGUE

*We must not give what we have but
we must give what we are!*

-Joseph Mercier

Serving and helping others will never
be outdated. It is a part of the very fabric
of life itself. One does not have to be
a psychologist to recognize the advantages
in spiritual growth and understanding that
is realized by an open mind, a generous
heart and a posture of loving service toward
others — compared to a selfish attitude
with self-interest being the primary focus.

We were all created in the image and
likeness of God. As such, we have, deep
within us, the drive to extend and apply
our Creator's love and forgiveness to every

creature. After all, everyone created by God is a member of God's Family.

There are so many ways to serve. Most often, our families are closest to us...which means they are the most vulnerable! It is easy to hurt the people we love and who share the home in which we live.

At the same time, our efforts of serving are almost non-stop! Every day the spouse or the children feel the joy of loving and being loved through acts of kindness, care and trust. Relatives and friends share the same expectation of being treated with loving concern. The opposite is devastating!

Sometimes we forget to use some important words, such as, "I love you.", or "Thank you." or "Is there anything I can do to help?"

We forget to pray for one another. Once we have come to the realization that God is our Divine Parent and we are all siblings to one another, how is it possible to ignore one another? The color of our skin, our language or our belief system may differ, but point to anyone on this planet and I will show you your brother or your sister.

I have merely offered in this book a taste of what a labor of love is like when it stems from our heart and soul. There are no exceptions. We all have the desire of being happy. We also have daily opportunities to test Tagore's wonderful secret to happiness. Every day! It may be through actions, prayers, happy thoughts or a letter written from the heart to console a sick person.

I have presented some ideal situations; however, I am not excluding the *Law of Failability!* I am not excluding our general purpose for being here on planet Earth for a certain period of time. Sickness, disease and death respect no one! They are simply a sign that our work is done ...or perhaps there is a lesson to learn if the condition continues for many years.

This is not the Kingdom of God. Living is learning by experience.

God offers each member of His Divine Family — you and me — support, strength and guidance through the Holy Spirit. In good times and in difficult times, God's Presence and Help are ever present. You are never alone! The One Who gave you life is ever at your side, and as the poet says, sometimes walking with you and sometimes carrying you — and as I believe — sometimes *pushing* you.

To order additional copies of "My Greatest Joys on My Way Home", or any of the other books by Rev. Jay Samonie, complete the information below.

Mail to: (Please print)

Name_____

Address_____

City, State, Zip

Phone (_____)_____

Copies of "My Greatest Joys on

My Way Home" @ $14.95

Michigan tax @ .90 per book_____

Shipping and handling @ $3.00_____

    Total amount enclosed $_____

Make checks payable to:

        Rev. Jay Samonie

     34666 Spring Valley Dr.

     Westland, MI 48185-9457